Caleb and Me

Down's Syndrome through a Father's eyes

Caleb and Me

Down's Syndrome through a Father's eyes

George Moody

Caleb and Me
by George Moody

Copyright © 2020 by George Moody

ISBN 979-86-38349-68-4

All right reserved

2nd Edition

CONTENTS

INTRODUCTION

A few years ago I became deeply upset. My government had introduced a new test for Down's Syndrome that allowed women to discover earlier and more safely if the child they carried had the extra chromosome. And everyone in politics and the medical profession seemed to hail it as a wonderful new treatment. But it wasn't a treatment at all. It was a form of pre-natal genocide. From now on no child need be born with Down's Syndrome. We were to eradicate this affliction from our country, from our planet. Such a view was so at odds with my experience of living with Caleb, I had to write about it. His life was not a curse to anyone, not to himself, not to us, not to those who met him. Quite the contrary. His life was a blessing to everyone with whom he came in contact. He changed the world and everyone in it for the better. Oh, I'm not pretending it is easy to love a child with additional needs. It is not. But that's rather the point. If we eliminate anyone that makes life a bit tricky where would we stop. So I wrote. I sat down and put on paper all the stories about him I loved so much. And it turned into a book. And that was nearly it, but three people did simple things to encourage me. Mark at BRF loved it and wanted it published but, as with every other publisher, it didn't fit. Celia said try Amazon self publish, it's easy. And Andy. Well, Andy did so much it is impossible to explain, but he checked, edited, encouraged and blessed. And he still does. So thanks to each. And thanks to Alison, who must wonder what I do all day, but loves me anyway, and puts up with finding her way into the pages of this book. I hope it blesses you too.

Caleb Appears

Low light, hard walls and a silent hole around the bed as white coated women whisper in the surrounding gloom. A special birth. Well, all births are special. It's just that some births are more special than others.

We should have known that it would not go to plan. For one, there was a plan. This was a little unusual for us. We are last minute people. We have to organise in reverse, as a kind of backwards engineering of life, assuming there was a plan even though we were not party to it. This time, though, the diary had actually appeared - and almost had some real writing in it. The birth was to be in late September, and my wife, Alison, would take the three weeks after school had started to get everything ready for the new arrival.

For two, I had been praying particularly hard. Not on my knees, you understand, as I did not go in much for kneeling then. But I had a particular prayer. Dear Lord, make this child healthy in mind, body and spirit. It seemed a silly selfish prayer even then, but it arose out of a deep fear. I did not want a disabled son. This stemmed, I think, from a ferry crossing to France, or somewhere thereabouts. My colleague was marking exam papers – totally against the rules – and I was free from distraction. Then this young man started to call out. Mad, meaningless noises came from his mouth – or so it seemed to me. Don't give me a disabled son, Lord, or at least that is what I thought I was praying, but somehow I could not bring myself to ask for that.

Then the big giveaway came on our end of holiday walk. The sun was shining, the bees were buzzing, the children were actually walking without fussing and then it came. The first pains. And it was still August.

Now Alison is not great at listening to her own body. When I am shivering on the sofa and my lips are turning blue with cold, she is off upstairs turning the thermostat down because it's too hot. Likewise, when training for the London Marathon, she ran around the same New Haven block thirteen times. This is the USA. On Sunday. Not a car, not a person, not even a dog was out to relieve the boredom, but she just kept on running. I would have been singing nursery rhymes and drooling after about 5 minutes, as my brain turned to slush from the monotony.

She is particularly not great at listening to her own body when it comes to childbirth. For our first, she was in bed with a stopwatch timing her contractions to the nearest second.

'Was that 33 or 34 seconds, darling. We can only go when it reaches 32.'

'We're going...now.'

For the second, she would have given birth in the elevator, if it had not come at once. In a normal hospital, she probably would have produced right there on the floor, but this one was due for replacement. The Beirut-style holes in the wall and absence of porters commandeering the lifts were surprisingly signs that things were going in our favour. The place was practically deserted, so that no one was there to slow us down.

More than that, if it had not been a Sunday, our first-born son would most certainly have appeared into this world on the back seat of the car. A journey that normally took forty-minutes had taken us only ten.

The third was at home. I'm usually rather squeamish, finding the amazing quantities of blood at birth only surpassed in horror-inducing effect by the, to me bizarre, requirement that I cut the cord. For those yet to have this pleasure it's surprisingly like cutting raw chicken. And surprisingly disgusting. However, in the interests of getting to the right place at the right time, I thought the living room was safer than the hospital. If previous records were anything to go by, this one would come out as if shot from a gun. So it would prove, but even this rapid expulsion of baby did not stop Alison taking a telephone call half way through. I'm not sure now if the friend ever knew but it was a strange sight to see your wife sitting on the sofa having a chat about nothing, while two mid-wives look on quietly deciding which one was about to play catch with our child.

Now the pains on the walk were not, according to Alison, 'real contractions'. So we were just going to the hospital to be 'checked out'. As an experienced husband, I was saying nothing, or at least the equivalent of 'yes, dear' for my generation. Never contradict your wife, is the unspoken rule – unless it's a matter of life or death, or you've found a way of saving money of course. Certainly never when it comes to children, washing up, cleaning, clothes, shopping, almost anything, in fact. But very particularly anything that might come under the heading Women's Matters – though even this is open to a surprisingly wide definition. So to hospital we went, for a 'check up'. They knew better, which was when it seemed to start to go wrong.

At first, it was the loss of three weeks preparation time that hit us most. This birth was going to be just right and now it was just wrong. They say the loss of anticipated pleasures can hit particularly hard. Somehow the human psyche is hard-wired to live more in the future than the present so that the absence of a hoped for event can have greater impact even than a present loss. So it was for us. Until, that is, Baby Moody actually appeared.

He was beautiful from the first. Beautiful but slightly odd looking. Every feature in place, every element perfectly symmetrical, just slightly different. Alison knew immediately. What tuned me in were the quiet whispers, just off camera.

The doctor marched in brimming with confidence. Somehow that helped more than anything that could have been said or done. She showed us how he differed. Look here, she said, he's floppy. Look here, his features are underdeveloped across the middle of his face. And look here is a classic feature, he has an extra-large gap between his big toe and the rest of his foot.

I've loved that gap ever since. When he was younger he used to park his rice-cakes in that gap, to keep them ready, for later. These days, if I get hold of his foot, I stroke the gap. It's my sign that he is special, unique, mine.

To my surprise, and I think to the undying admiration of the delightful, if slightly dizzy, midwife, I never felt any sense of fear or rejection. This beautiful child was mine and he was perfect. I would love him whatever happened and however hard that became. What was immediately apparent, though, was that this one would be different. From the off, he would require more help and support from outside the home than all the other three put together. Once we counted thirteen professionals specifically on his case. But he was different in another way. He was healthy in mind, body and spirit. Where the others had got ill, he did not. Where the others had struggled with friendship groups, he did not. Where the others had been variously happy, sad, joyful, miserable, he was not. A healthier, happier, more well-balanced child I have never met.

He did not have a name at first, but when it came it was a big one. Alison was the first to suggest Baby Moody should become Caleb, but I immediately knew it was right. Caleb had been Joshua's faithful companion who led his people into the promised land. So our Caleb was to lead our family into a land 'flowing with milk and honey', a new and better way to live as family. And so he has. But he has done something rather more than that, for one of the first realisations for me was simple, but life-changing. If he had appeared into almost any family other than our own, he would not have been allowed to live. He would have died in the womb and never made it into this world. This amazing character who brings sunshine to everyone he meets, who is loved by everyone he knows, would never have seen the light of day. And that thought has changed me. If that can happen, something is not right.

In a very real sense that is what this book is about. It's not only about Caleb but about the insight his life can give into the others who have never been able to live in our world. It's about the other Calebs who are not among us. I've called them the womb-dwellers.

It is also about us. All of us. Not in any sense judgmentally. Not a chance to criticise or complain. Merely a chance to examine. For Caleb somehow changes people. They, like me, are often afraid, and like me, when Caleb appears, their fear disappears. This book hopes similarly to bring change. To enable people like you and me to seek a better future. A way out of a world that rejects as unworthy of life those whom we seem most to need to be alive, those who have the greatest chance of making our world a better place.

It is also about ideas. I make no excuses for this. It is no revelation that ideas matter in our world. They may even shape it. But more than that, on this issue in particular, new ideas matter, because the old ideas have become stale. We seem stuck in opposing camps, without a way across the divide. This book hopes to offer a bridge big enough to dwell on and wide enough to allow all to travel on. You can, of course, skip the ideas, but I hope you won't, because without them I do not think there is any way forward.

Beginnings

Nine months before Caleb's birth something extraordinary happened. I am not referring, you understand, to the event that occurs nine months before any birth. That event, as many husbands will confirm, may well be quite unusual, especially once you are married with young children. Mind you even the connection between that common event and the birth of a baby does seem to take some by surprise. I vividly remember standing in a car park in Dorset quietly observing the Rude Man of Cern (who, it is worth noting for readers of Victorian guidebooks, does *not* wear a loin cloth), when a late middle aged woman came up to me and remarked on how her daughter had been helped to conceive by sitting on part of the Rude Man (or, more accurately the Rude Man's parts). 'She must have been doing something else, as well,' was my rapid, if slightly predictable reply. I only mention it, of course, to highlight the fact that in matters of reproduction people seem often to come over a bit odd. It's almost as if the connection between activities in bed and the arrival of a screaming infant have become so forgotten in our modern world that people find it slightly embarrassing to put the two together.

As I was saying, nine months before Caleb's birth something even more unusual happened. A cell divided in order to produce a special cell designed for reproduction, but instead of leaving exactly half the normal number of chromosomes, it left one extra copy of chromosome 21. Other than the almost redundant X-chromosome, which by its inadequacy produces us men, chromosome 21 is by far the smallest of all the chromosomes in the human cell. What exactly it does is beyond the scope of this book, and the wisdom of this writer (it may be beyond anyone's understanding actually as the interaction between genes is unbelievably complicated), but it certainly does something. I vaguely feel that it just makes everything a bit smaller than it would be otherwise. Certainly Caleb's tubes are all a little minuscule, from the one that runs through his body, to the passages of his nose, to, possibly, the nerve cells that run his brain, which may account for the slowing of his thought processes. But whatever it does, it's pretty major. If it were any other chromosome that had doubled up, he would never have survived the womb.

One thing the extra chromosome does not affect is the new cell's ability to swim. Or at least it does not stop it winning a long distance swimming race with over a hundred million of its kind. Through the porthole, across the ocean and even up the channel it goes, tail twisting, head forging forward. Only one can win. In this case it's a special one. Of course, to describe this cell as swimming is a little generous. It is more like a torpedo than a fish. It has an engine and a packet to deliver, and quite an explosive packet it proves to be, transforming its target beyond recognition. As the charge goes off deep inside a vessel vastly bigger than itself, two sets of chromosomes, half from each parent, recombine to form an entirely new entity, almost alien, utterly unexpected, a total transformation from the old. And so our story really begins. The womb dweller has arrived.

Why 'womb dweller'? Well, please allow me a brief aside. It's about names. In the UK, Dennis is not a very common name. I suspect this is because many of us were brought up on Dennis the Menace, and, though we loved his mischief, we did not want to have a Dennis in our homes. Naughty children can be quite amusing, but only if you do not like their parents. In the USA, however, Dennis is a reasonably common name. According to a 2001 report nattily entitled *Why Susie Sells Seashells by the Seashore: Implicit Egotism and Major Life Decisions*, in that year it ranked 40th between Jerry (39th) and Walter (41st). So, when it comes to members of certain professions, you would expect roughly the same order in frequency of names. However, there is one profession where the ratings are a little skewed. You've guessed it. Dennis is destined to be a dentist. While in the dentist world there were 257 Walters and 270 Jerrys, 482 Dennises had chosen the profession.

So names matter and may even decide our future but when it comes to the womb they matter a lot. This is partly because the ones we've got are so unappealing. Of the common ones fetus (or foetus, if you're picky) is clearly the contents of a particularly nasty boil, embryo is a make of child's plastic toy, blastocyst is a military ordinance of minute size and massive power, and conceptus is the new name of a public limited company dreamed up by a firm of overpaid management consultants. Not one of them contains the concept of life (except possibly the fetid pus), which is the fundamental feature of this new being. He is human and he is alive. He has a full complement of human DNA, even with extra copies, lucky thing, and he is going to grow pretty fast pretty soon. And in a few days he will be looking for a comfortable bed to lie on. Hold on a minute, though, for that will come later. First, we must replay the last few sentences slowly.

He? Well 'it' will not do, as the diminutive X-chromosome denotes gender, and while we might hope there is more to maleness than a lack of size in one department, it cannot be denied that it is pretty significant. Even my children's pets have gender. I once discovered my chimney had gender ('a lovely chimney, she be'), which may be going a bit far, but my womb dweller must be male.

Human? This is not really in dispute. The womb dweller is human for what else can he be? But is he human like me, sitting, washed and well fed, or is he human like the skin cells under my armpit, which I slough off in the bath? The answer, of course, is neither. Personally, I will be persuaded that the womb dweller is like the skin cell under my armpit when I see a baby growing there. Technology may one day allow an armpit cell to be converted into a womb dweller, but then it will no longer be an armpit cell – it will be a womb dweller.

It is much closer to say that he is like me for he shares with me the status of individual. Just as there can never be another of me, so there can never be another of him. Slightly oddly one could become two. In these first few days, there could be a split in the ball of cells to make two womb dwellers, two new individuals, each with unique experiences from first to last. But both before and after they are individuals, first one, then two (or even in rare cases back to one again.)

If you doubt that all are individuals, follow me on a little thought experiment. If, in some future world it was possible to clone me, to make a new copy of me from a cell of my body, would that make the old, pre-clone me, less of an individual? Would the split from one individual into two mean either had less value. It seems unlikely. If it did it would certainly lead to most interesting consequences. 'Bored with your old model. Madam? Scrap him and grow a new one from scratch. Better still trade him in for spare parts. You could even keep them on ice for when the new version starts to wear out.'

No, the major difference between him and me is size. He's just rather smaller, indeed approximately a quadrillion times smaller. This fact rather reduces his ability to do a lot of other things, but none of these are things that time will not solve, if only he is given time. For unlike our popular image of the womb, it is not a safe place to be for this new individual human life.

On April 13th 1970, the Apollo 13 mission suffered a catastrophic explosion that ruptured an oxygen tank, causing the loss of all power in the command module. From that moment on, the mission turned from making a third landing on the moon to a desperate attempt to rescue the three astronauts, James Lovell,

Jack Swigert and Fred Haise. It is an astonishing story of courage and cleverness, which made a fabulous film starring Tom Hanks. For me the most poignant moment is not the initial battle to survive or the long planning required to bring them back to earth. No, it is that final moment when they are in reach of the atmosphere, in sight of home and it is revealed that they must make one last burn of the engines, manually, without the help of the computer. If they make one small mistake, the craft will skip off the earth's atmosphere like a stone skimming on a pond and rebound back into space to be lost adrift for eternity. It is the perfect 'so close yet so far' moment of film history.

Now spare a thought for our new womb dweller. So far he is not home but floating down the fallopian tube, growing exponentially, but without any outside source of nourishment. He must land on the womb wall or drift off into nothing. It is his first hurdle and it is quite a biggy. If the timing is not right the landing site will not be perfectly prepared. If the hormones are wrong then there may be nothing to land on, or he may be expelled, with no hope of a second chance.

Our womb dweller is one of the fortunate ones. All is ready and welcoming. A safe landing. Now he may start to flourish. Many are not so lucky. Estimates vary but it is thought that up to half of his kind may miss this first target by natural processes. And that probably does not include those summarily ejected by a massive hormone dose that is deliberately used to flush him out.

At this stage we adults are none the wiser about this extraordinary event. There are a few more days at least of that period of married life known as trying for a baby. This is a sunshine moment for any man who does not suffer from an allergy to children. There is no cry of 'headache, darling' or a mumbled 'too tired'. Not even a 'not now, the children may hear', which seems to cover just about any eventuality including between the hours of midnight and five in the morning. There is no need for flowers, chocolates, or considerate offers to wash up or take out the recycling. It's all go, and the only desire not satisfied is for your wife to be in that perfect zone where she is fertile enough to have children, but not fertile enough for it to happen anytime too soon, thus avoiding the misery of infertility and enjoying the pleasure of regular practice. Sadly it does not last long. Alison is regular as clockwork and any gap is a sure fire sign that a baby is on the way, and so it proves. The womb dweller has arrived, and he will be surprisingly dominant for much of the next nine months, though not nearly as surprisingly dominant as he is once he comes out.

Occasionally in family life, everything goes your way. A few weeks back I had one of those days. My middle son was away with his cousin in London. Alison had taken my daughter shopping with her friends in Bath, which was a double blessing. I had been left behind with only the shortest to do list and I was missing out on a shopping trip. This left my eldest son who promptly decided that being at home all day with Dad was pretty dull and rang up a friend. He would not be home for hours. So Caleb and I had the day to ourselves.

It began with a game of bed sharks. I am not sure if you are aware but large double beds can become infested with sharks, who eat, or at least attempt to eat, the feet of unsuspecting children while they are comfortably squatting on their parents' pillows. Ours was suffering an especially bad infestation and Caleb could not risk poking even the tiniest toe under the duvet. Every nifty nip was accompanied by howls of laughter and a quick escape to another section of pillow, only for a surreptitious return a few moments later in the hope of another nip from nimble fingers. It could have gone on all day if breakfast had not called to the larger person's larger stomach.

It was a beautiful spring day, fine, bright and surprisingly warm. On such a day Caleb insists on a trip to the trampoline. This used to be called the 'bounce-ween', which was always kind of cute and a rather better name than the correct one. On it there are many family games, including 'roll', which involves attempts to squash him by rolling across the trampoline, and 'bounce' which is an excuse to throw him high up into the air, but his favourite is 'food'. Daddy says a rhyme which goes, 'I like toes for breakfast. I like toes for tea. I like toes for supper. Now bring those toes here to me.' At each line, I have to chase him around the trampoline on hands and knees, never quite catching up until with a final lunge, I am expected to throw myself at his feet in the vain hope of getting a bite of toe. Occasionally the verse is further enhanced with the addition of other menus, such as toes on toast, or toe sausages, but the game is ever the same, and always produces peals of laughter and ecstatic runnings around the edge of the mat to escape the encompassing jaws.

Afterwards I made him lunch. This was a typically Daddy treat: the banned chocolate spread sandwich, juice rather than water and never at the table. It was a 'mummy's out' moment, if ever there was one. At the end he turned to me as I sat next to him on the bench outside and said, 'Dadda is best friend.' As ways of making Daddy happy it was, and remains, unbeatable. Compared to what he gave me that day, with those few words, I had given so little. It was certainly a day to remember.

It was also a moment for contemplation. It struck me that it was entirely natural for me, as a Dad, to lavish such attention on my son. It felt right in every way. I was there not so much to 'spoil' my son but to 'special' him, to provide the 'upgrade' on life, as my children would call it. And I sensed that this came about because I was always playing catch up. Alison had had exclusive access, undivided attention, for the first nine months of human life, putting me forever an age behind. While he had been the womb dweller, she had been the womb maker, as for those months of life and development, his life and hers had been more closely linked than was ever possible again. What she ate, he tasted. Where she walked he followed, probably asleep, so that when she stopped, he became active, getting himself ready to party as she tried to rest. If she became ill, his life was at even greater threat than hers. If he became ill, her life was at risk alongside his. If either were to become at odds with the other, then both could die. And if, at the last moment of womb dwelling something should go wrong, then those nine months were the only moments they could ever share together, with me forever left outside. Even now, even today, even in the best hospital in the world, both could die in one ghastly moment of time, leaving behind a devastation possibly unparalleled in personal human loss.

For now our womb dweller is safe, a rapidly growing ball of cells, like a tiny football. Often this is used against him. He is described as 'just' a ball of cells, conveniently ignoring that the speaker is 'just' a funny-shaped tube of cells. Is it shape that counts? Is a more rounded person less valuable than a more angular person? It might suggest that the quiet little belly that I have acquired as a rather feeble form of middle-aged spread has somehow reduced my significance in the world. Maybe it has. It certainly gives Alison and children something to tease me about, though that seems to me a good thing. Or maybe it is the type of cells that counts? My cells are all different while for the moment his are pretty much all the same. But this just makes the early womb dweller more valuable. These special cells are often hailed as the great new cure for disease and infirmity. Anyway, a value based on how useful you are to science is more than a little horrifying. Shall we harvest you for your unusual blood group, like a maple tree that is sucked of its sap? Fine if you have my permission, but the womb dweller cannot give permission, and is rather unlikely to do so if it means the end of his existence.

Some might want to compare him to an acorn, that may grow if planted, but has no real value in itself, while we are mighty oaks, which are to be treasured and protected. Unfortunately, this conveniently forgets that one reason we value the oak more highly than the acorn is that we can chop it down for wood. It also should not be forgotten that saplings in our neat suburban gardens are ruthlessly ripped from the ground. If humans were treated in any way like oaks and acorns, we would be culling children who ended up in the wrong place and harvesting convenient adults for organs. It is one way forward, I suppose, but is unpleasantly reminiscent of the misery of village poverty in northern India, where adult organs are harvested and children are sold into bonded labour.

No, we must value our womb dweller for himself and not seek comparisons. Particularly as there is nothing like him. He's only been with the womb maker for 3 weeks and already he's pumping his own blood, more like a jet engine whine than her rhythmically beat, but nevertheless it's going around carrying nutrients provided by her to every part of his growing body. She may only just be aware of the possibility of his existence and already he is establishing the beginnings of independence. Within a week he may even find some comfort in his watery home by sucking his thumb as he floats free.

Another month goes by and he begins to swim rather than float, a perfectly formed miniature version of the womb maker, merely a centimetre long, but with finely tapering fingers, delicate ears and clear, closed eyes. The tiny electrical impulses pinging off all these sensitive parts now have a home to go to as the brain starts to form in all its astonishing complexity. As the womb maker listens to rock so the womb dweller inside her rocks to the beat. As she eats curry so he tastes the spice. As she rests and delights, so he grows and enjoys. And while no one can recall the womb, it is while in the womb that root memories may be laid down to determine much of his future.

As she is, so is he, in harmony or in hatred, in hope or in anguish, in delight or even in disgust, the two are bound together as one. For after only a couple more months of intimacy, she will be asked to choose, nay recommended, to rid herself of his flawed self. Thankfully for Alison and me, we had made our choice long before, so we never asked to know. For others it is a terrible dilemma. Take the test, check the scan, he looks abnormal, have the procedure. How can anyone choose under such pressure? Some friends were put through this mangle, were told their daughter would be different. They resisted and rejected the advice to destroy her only to find out at her birth that she had no disability at all.

But more of this later. For now our womb dweller is safe, protected and cosseted in a sack of fluid, a space capsule that provides the perfect environment. He has passed the major danger period, and, after six months, begins to practice breathing, drawing in fluid through his nose and mouth. His body remains ideally suited to his current environment, with special downy hair covering him all over and a ridged feeding tube through his stomach, but he must get ready to go out. He begins to open those perfect closed eyes, to listen more carefully and respond to his mother's voice, even to begin to hiccup as his diaphragm gets used to unexpected activity. He would not easily survive yet without her protection, but he would have a jolly good try, and, with huge help and fate and fortune on his side, he might just make it, out in the fresh air.

Now, finally, he will begin to make his presence fully felt, pushing a hand, a foot or an elbow against his soft and yielding walls. His father is woken to see a lump crossing his wife's belly so that Dad is inevitably reminded of the Alien movies, where the creature explodes from its host's stomach, and of the final scene of the Matrix, where Mr Smith's face bubbles then ruptures from the inside as Neo wins through. This is not something to mention, of course, as delight is the only acceptable emotion, but it can rather emphasise the isolation Dad may feel from the inner being, the womb dweller, even while it is that first wondrous moment of a beginning relationship.

In Caleb's case none of this happened. There was no first movement, no kick of quickening, no visible hint of the coming invasion. He was wonderfully placid in the womb, the model dweller, giving his mother no trouble. But of course this should have given us cause for concern. When I was in my first teaching job, I became good friends with a colleague whose first child suffered from a very serious congenital disorder which caused her to steadily decline over a number of years, to an early death. We spoke much about it, as I sought to support him in the only way I knew, by being aware, and in time I was able to share a little in his happiness when his second child was born. I had, of course, to ask the inevitable question, though you could see by his face what was the answer. Was she alright?

'We knew immediately,' was his calm reply, 'because she cried.' It was the difficulty of dealing with a crying baby that made it clear she was well, not the ease of a placid one. So with Caleb. While he has given us his share of trouble, in those weeks leading up to his birth, he was the easiest of babies. I am not, you understand, suggesting that carrying a baby is ever easy. The womb maker has her work cut out just to get through the nine months of pregnancy, let alone the hours or days of labour. But in relative terms, Caleb was easy. He was easy even on the way out. A couple of pushes and out he popped.

I've recently noticed that having babies is quite competitive. It is generally second hand suffering. "Did you hear that Angela was in labour for five days.' (She's certainly not too posh to push, then.) 'Really, Jen was in for five days and then had gas and air and an epidural. Even then they had to pull the baby out with a wrench.' 'Well, our cousin Steph went off to the loo and out popped the baby' (At least she didn't have to wash it). 'Really, Pat had hers in her slippers as she got into bed.' I'm not sure if it's a sisterhood solidarity thing, or it's a rather less than subtle form of one-up-man-ship, but, men, don't whatever you do try to join in, or you'll be jeered at for being a weakling when it comes to pain and cut down with a phrase that starts, 'If men had babies...' I always want to say 'but men do stupid things and get injured all the time – we know quite a lot about pain' but it's always best to keep quiet. It is a moment of female glory that should never be taken away.

Anyway, that dangerous aside over, out comes the baby, now no longer a womb dweller, but an air dweller like you and me. He is about to live on the outside, ready or not. In Caleb's case it was a week in hospital with his mother, sorting out his jaundice. Nevertheless it is now time. Now suddenly, he is no longer at risk from the womb maker, but must face the world. Is it a place of danger or of welcome? We will find out soon, but first we must return to those womb dwellers who have not been so lucky, to those for whom life ends early, and the industry that benefits.

The Waiting Room

My mother tells a story of going in for an examination. As you will immediately understand, this was not exactly a written test, and involved the examiner getting a view rarely seen in polite society. It was in hospital and so she went through the usual dehumanising routine of getting out of her normal clothes into an open-backed gown, lying back on a padded pallet, and resting with her knees up – at which point the doctor walks in. Now, this was in the days when doctors could find themselves a bit more insulated from their patients than they are today, and she had no clue as to who would be coming through the door. It is rather understating it to reveal that she was less than happy to find the smiling face of a parent of a pupil at my father's school staring at her from between her legs. It was not so much that she did not like him. Previously they had got on well and, a little unexpectedly, he kept up a pleasant and jolly conversation about school life during the rest of the examination. It was just that she was not sure she'd be able to look him in the face again, without remembering where he had been looking not long before.

For him, it was routine, normal, everyday. For her it was personal, private and intimate. And as we enter the 'family planning' clinic waiting room we cannot help be struck that this is the real problem with all that is said and done with the womb-dweller and the womb maker. For them it is the most personal of personal moments. For others it has become another matter altogether, a fight for control. Much of this we will touch on later, but at this point it is important to recognise that adding further to the attempts to control women is not the purpose of this book. Men (and women) have done quite enough of that already and I have no desire to add to it. Neither is this an attempt at a masculine view. Personally I am not sure gender is quite such a control of character as everyone seems to think, but even if it is, all a masculine view would do would be to add to the way in which some control others. No, this book is just about how these things affect Caleb and me. It's about a father and his son – his beloved, youngest son – Caleb Benjamin.

Another room, another examination. This time everyone has his or her clothes on (he, his and her, hers, of course). It would have certainly changed the atmosphere if we had decided to meet naked (the window would have been closed anyway) but fortunately it was not on the agenda. A tiny room and a large table surrounded by those shrunken chairs you only find in primary schools. Peculiarly uncomfortable for anyone over five foot, but bearable in these circumstances. What would strike anyone who came into that room is how extraordinarily positive and purposeful everyone is. There's almost a party atmosphere. It may be because a number of the participants are getting a morning off school to be there, but there's more to it than that. It's more as if they are being allowed, for once, to do what they got into teaching to do, to really focus on the wellbeing of one pupil. They are being given a whole hour to talk about Caleb.

By the time the room is full there are nearly a dozen of us: teaching staff, special educational needs coordinator (SENCO), professionals and parents. Each has their own role, some to contribute plans, some to offer insight, some to report on progress, some to listen. It is structured, careful, directed and very hopeful. And by the end Caleb's education has been minutely dissected and everyone, including his largely ignorant parents have had a chance to contribute. The meeting has all but broken up and then comes the moment to remember.

'You do realise', says the SENCO, 'that Caleb is the hero of the school.'

'Everyone knows Caleb,' he goes on, 'especially after he became the good Samaritan'.

It was a good story, and worth re-telling. The older children had been practising a play of the story of the Good Samaritan. They had just got to the part where the traveller gets beaten up by robbers. The girl playing the victim was lying on the ground in a metaphorical pool of blood, just as Caleb is passing to go to class. The story is that he left the line and crossed the hall so as to help her up, to rescue her from her attackers. It is clear that he did not realise it was a play. What is also then clear is that he was willing to step into a group of children attacking another child and protect her. The headmaster delightedly made much of it, with a presentation in assembly (which Caleb thinks of as a present, of course, and he loves presents), and a story retold at every opportunity – Caleb, the hero of the school.

Occasionally, we do our duty to the Down's Syndrome movement by attending one of their conferences. We're not particularly keen to get too heavily involved. We have this vague idea that doing too much in a group of parents of children with Down's Syndrome emphasises Caleb's differentness, and for us he is always just Caleb. Of course, we are hugely grateful for all the support and try to give something back, though it's rare these days that we get involved. Anyway, it was the usual mix of the marvellous and the well meaning, but one moment sticks in my mind. A parent of a much older girl gave a talk on his experience of having a child with Down's Syndrome at a mainstream secondary school. For him the greatest fear was that she would be bullied for being different. According to him nothing was further from the truth. She found herself, as expected, in all the bottom groups, with the troubled boys, who were prone to aggression and abuse of others. However, what happened was that, far from picking on her, they protected her.

'Here was someone,' he said, 'who was worse at Maths than they were.'

She was no threat at all. It was her very disability, her very vulnerability that made her someone to be valued and loved. She did not judge and find wanting. She valued friendship and nothing else. Jean Vanier, founder of L'Arche, says the same thing about when he first met two friends with learning difficulty. Unlike his philosophy students, who were only interested in ideas, these two men had one question, 'When will we see you again?' All they were interested in was relationship.

When I first realised that Caleb would have many brothers, many more with the same disability as him, if it were not for abortion, what struck me was the immense loss. 'Everyone needs a Caleb' I kept saying. And it seems to me to be true. We all need someone more vulnerable, more needy than ourselves or we have no one to care for, except our selves. "Whosoever preserves a single soul of Israel, Scripture ascribes to him as if he had preserved a complete world" says the Talmud (or 'save one soul, save the world entire' as Spielberg has it). For Caleb and me it is rather, 'Lose one soul, lose the world entire'. What would the world be like if every family had a Caleb? Tired and poor, you might say, and you'd probably be right (more of that later), but I'm willing to bet there would be very few wars, very little oppression, and a great deal of loving care. Now I must get off my soapbox and back into the waiting room.

A different waiting room, eighteen months before Caleb's birth. This time Alison is on her own, waiting – waiting to see the doctor. I rather like this doctor. For me as a bloke, he's ideal. You go in, he takes one look at you, he writes out a prescription, you go away. No prodding, no searching questions, just a gruff jovial voice, a vague sense that he's recently broken off from a round of golf, and a rapid expulsion into the outside world. There's not even a wait. For me, virtually perfect. Not so for Alison. His opening words are

'We'd better deal with the miscarriage first'

Now if you're a woman reading this, there'll have been a sharp intake of breath and probably a sub-audible 'poor thing'. If you're a man, you might have a vague sense that there's something wrong, but little more. And here we have the problem. However carefully they place pot plants and pictures, magazines and mini motorcars, a waiting room is always going to be a place where something is about to be done to you. It is here, where you are initiated into the process of passivity, awaiting someone else to act. Your choice has been made as soon as you enter and the action done, however violent, is inevitable. In the abortion clinic, it is always a woman who is the visible recipient and usually, at least in this part of the world, a man who acts. Does it feel like the gentle caress of a lover, or the violent violation of a rapist? Who knows but the one who goes. On this others have more right than I to speak, but what I do know is how Alison felt on receiving that doctor's words and 'violated' does it little justice. The moment of quiet tragedy was stomped all over, and with boots worthy of a giant.

I recently travelled to visit a very special organisation, called Care Confidential. Their mandate is to help women who are going through the process of abortion. They do not judge. They do not preach. They do not prevent. They aim merely to protect women. I even tested them against the antennae of a group of pupils. They came out as the one unbiased group. Oddly, in some ways however, they are entirely biased. They hope that women will choose not to proceed with abortion, which makes their work all the more fascinating. How can a group be both entirely supportive of women involved in abortion and entirely against abortion itself. By the end of my visit I think I understood. I discovered two things. The first surprised me. In their experience it was rarely the womb maker who wanted the abortion. Of course sometimes it was, but more usually it was those around her. The 'supportive' boyfriend. The 'concerned' mother. The 'honest' friend. Most women offering for abortion felt powerless to do otherwise.

Not only that but the only person who really suffers after an abortion is the womb maker who has had her womb emptied. Their experience was that everyone else forgot almost immediately and suffered no adverse emotional reactions at all. This rang true with my experience. I was, to my shame, just like the doctor who had so little apparent concern for Alison. I never felt any direct sorrow about the lost child. Nor even, I have to confess, did I wonder much about what was lost. Until that is Caleb appeared. And then I understood. It was probably genetics that caused the loss. Some greater fault than Caleb's. Possibly even another doubled chromosome, as any other would have resulted in death fairly rapidly. Caleb became even more a miracle and Alison's sorrow became more real. You see, it is the womb maker that suffers. All the rest of us are onlookers. But that doesn't mean that we can look on without care.

Another room. Still clinical but this time smaller. Still waiting, but not for a doctor. She has already been and done. Now we're waiting for news.

'Slightly small for this stage of gestation but nothing to worry about. Have you had the test?'

The question comes out almost as if read from a script. It is not in itself a biased question, but its appearance unbidden is a bit of a surprise. You feel almost guilty in the reply,

'We're not having the test'

There's no comeback, but we are clearly abnormal. Most have the test. Even friends and family who we know are vocally opposed to abortion have the test. 'It's better to know. At least you can prepare.' What, by painting the walls a different colour?

What seems to be clear is that successive governments have made it increasingly easy to get tested and even easier to take the next step. A moderately costly procedure is often offered for free, presumably so that the state does not have to bear the cost of caring for a disabled child later. It is hard not to feel therefore that the state would really rather Caleb did not exist, however kindly and supportive are all those who help with his care. In one sense I don't care. 'Sod 'em' springs to mind. But it is hard not to feel that where the government and policy go first, there after goes everyone else. I know of friends who have been given quite a hard time in hospital for deigning to bring a disabled child into the world. 'Did you know?' I used to get asked, and almost felt guilty when I replied, 'No, we had no idea', because you could almost hear the sigh of relief. 'That's all right then. It's not their fault for bringing him into the world'. Of course it's my fault, I should cry, where do you think babies come from.

I remember early on finding myself running beside a member of the local running club (the bizarrely called 'Amblers') who had a disabled daughter. 'Yes,' he said, 'she's perfect.' It was as if a light went on in my head. I wouldn't change Caleb even if I could. He's perfect. And sod 'em if they think otherwise.

The first UK family planning clinic was opened by a woman called Marie Stopes on 17 March 1921. She was a wealthy, intelligent, educated, and highly academic (double first) successful author. In her first book, Married Love, she explores sexual relationships and birth control. While her ideas on the first were seen as revolutionary, suggesting (oh no) that women should enjoy sex, her ideas on the second were less well developed, arguing that you could prevent pregnancy if the man whipped it out half way through. It is amusing to reflect on how these two suggestions might be slightly contradictory.

Her second and more carefully crafted book, Wise Parenthood, deals with the subject of contraception. It is a fascinating little tome, not least because of its impact. Publicly vilified and personally attacked, often by clergy, she found herself weathering a storm of protest. On reading it, it is hard to see why, at least at first glance. Maybe it was the crude line drawing of a section across a womb and vagina (It looks more like a bird's eye view of a distorted estuary to me). Maybe it was the recommendation to a woman to place a cap over her cervix with her finger. The visual imagery this conjured up may have been too much for our priests to contemplate. Anyway it's hard to be sure, as it was too horrific for her opponents to go into details.

The only lines that appear surprising to my modern ears are those giving her reasons for contraception. At first sight the reason appears to be to make happy families, but it is not. It is something rather different. In her own words the man must feel a 'desire to repeat [his wife's] goodness and beauty through time' unless 'either is stricken by some inherent weakness' for 'children who descend from a line of healthy and intelligent parents are better equipped to face whatever difficulties may arise in their environment than children of unsound stock'.

Call me old fashioned but I have a slight problem with the suggestion that you should not breed if you come from 'unsound stock' particularly if the opposite to such 'stock' is health and intelligence. I am also not at all sure that 'repeating' Alison, beautiful though she is of course (let's hope she reads this), is the aim of reproduction. I naively thought it was love. What Marie Stopes had produced was a useful and informative little book, full of popular appeal, which appears, at least on the surface, to be an encouragement to genetic purification.

The first clinic was opened in Holloway. It is tempting to believe that the site was deliberately chosen to target the 'unsound stock' who were living in the newly developed poorer parts of North London, and I have certainly heard that accusation made. It is, of course, hard, if not impossible, to find evidence to support this view, though it would certainly fit her mission statement. What is clear is that from early on Marie Stopes both as an individual, and later as an organisation, exported her birth control policies with evangelical zeal, first across Britain and then to the rest of the world. In the last year for which I have records, Marie Stopes UK made a surplus of £35 million, much of which was used to set up clinics in, surprise, surprise, the very poorest and least educated parts of the world. Woe to you if you come from unsound stock.

It is also clear that, from the very first, Marie Stopes made no distinction between different methods of family planning, except on the effect it had on the pleasures involved in 'sex-relations' as she called them. There is a lovely piece in her book where she imagines the effect of *coitus interruptus* on the woman. She is waiting with bated breath to see if her man can get it out in time. She is crossing her fingers (though not, we hope, her legs) in anticipation of an early emission and any possible pleasure in the act is removed.

What the man is thinking is not touched on, of course.

I have noticed that this is a common approach among women, or at least one woman of my acquaintance.

'It's easy for you men,' she said, 'a couple of pushes, and you're done'

Skipping over, if we may, what is implied by the term 'couple', I found that comment a trifle unnerving. It implied that my only ambition in 'sex-relations' was to emit, and any desire for mutual pleasure was an annoyance. Now I know what the guru says, 'It takes two hands to clap', and am far happier when it works that way. But even if it doesn't, there's still the sheer terror of not keeping it up, the misery of everything happening far too fast, the unavoidable sense that someone is going to hold up score cards at the end, and the endless fumbling with those ridiculous rubber things just at the crucial moment. 'Easy,' I wanted to splutter, 'have you any idea how stressful it is to keep asking and getting turned down all the time, let alone the physical exertion required?' But of course, I didn't.

But, that risky interlude over and done with, back to Marie Stopes and our last waiting room. But some advice first. If you are easily grossed out, read no further. This waiting room is very small indeed. It is superbly designed and incredibly comfortable. No pot plants in sight and a décor that would grace Michael Jackson's boudoir. Here we have passivity at its most intense. Everything is received as a gift, with no possibility even of saying thank you. Nothing can be given back or re-paid. Here we have complete dependence, the most vulnerable of possible states. It's a long wait but well worth it, for outside the waiting room is a world full of possibilities. For now though we have only waiting.

'What's this?' An invader in the room, probing, searching, pushing, sucking. Now it sticks. Is it attached to an arm or a leg? The head maybe, though this is not its initial target. Then it pulls. To most people it would not be much of a pull, but to the one in the waiting room it is irresistible. And it does not pull them out into the air. No, it just pulls them apart. The leg, the arm, the pelvis, are yanked away and sucked out. Now for the head. But it's too big to get out so it must be crushed. Squeezed in pincers until it pops. Then the bits are dragged out and thrown in with the rest of the gory contents. A white cloth is gently folded over them, as if at this stage some belated respect is to be accorded to the small body parts before they are thrown in the fire.

It may be that the one who waits is unsound, as Caleb. Or it may be that he is unwanted, or that she is unexpected. It may even be that two is too many and one is just right. It may be that the mother is too young and the father is too foolish. Whatever the reason, the wait was in vain. The months of growing and preparing were for nothing. But this is no brief doctor's queue ending in a prescription and a trip to the pharmacy. This is the end of an eternal process, begun at the beginning of life, where, at the last, one set of genes is deemed unworthy of life.

Why, you might ask, all this maudlin misery? It's for one very simple reason. That waiting womb dweller could have been Caleb. I know that men are not meant to feel much. It's called lack of emotional intelligence. But I think this idea is entirely false. I think we feel very much – in fact often too much. It's just that it runs rather deep and is expressed rather shallow.

One of my friends was left at his boarding school age seven with these fatherly words,

'We don't kiss anymore son. Now we shake hands.'

He could still tell this story aged thirty-seven. It was a defining moment. Cruel? Probably. Did it mean his Dad did not love him? Definitely not. The thing about many men is that they just don't express the same emotions on the surface as they are feeling underneath. And this tends to strengthen the undercurrents.

Well the undercurrent for me is this,

'What if that had been Caleb?'

In four out of five families it would have been. I can almost see him being torn limb from limb, helpless and alone, and cannot imagine a world from which his smile is absent, a world in which his arms do not cuddle, a world in which I would never be called 'Dadda'.

In Hospital

Bright white linen and brilliant sunshine. Almost blinding. Hospital rooms shouldn't be like this. In this one there are two beds. One is a normal size, with those metallic bars that make hospital beds look like prison cells. The other is tiny. And raised up. It has a plastic dish on top, surprisingly like an enlarged version of those food-measuring bowls with the digital displays underneath. In this one there is no food but a small baby, our baby, Caleb.

He is a little green around the edges and has looming over him an array of blue-lit tubes. It's like he's on a sun-bed. It strikes me as a little odd that we're trying to give our newborn son a tan. Are we going to pretend we've just jetted in from Malaga with our newly adopted child, or something?

'What's that for?' I ask stupidly. You may have picked up by now that I'm not the brightest of husbands when it comes to anything not written down in front of me (or on a map of course – why is it that husbands cannot remember their wife's birthday but are excellent at finding Nether Wallop on a 1 cm to 1 mile map within a nanosecond of being asked?).

'He's just jaundiced.' Well that accounts for the greenness. He's really yellowish but the lights are blue so a ghastly green tinge is the result.

While this is all going on Ethan and Oliver have been exploring. Not the baby, as you might expect, but the facilities. Like most men they're more naturally drawn to stuff than people. Ethan has found the most exciting part of the room – the en-suite shower. At this point I want to remind you that this is a hospital and not a hotel. As our previous experience of babies and hospital was in the Beirut-homage building in Sheffield called the Jessop, just before it closed down, or was condemned, this one came as something of a surprise. Security had been tight. It felt like entering a spaceship rather than a ward. We had been processed through a kind of airlock, where we had to demonstrate our credentials. There was no retinal scanner but it would not have been out of place. And when we got through there was that marvellous hush that always accompanies real comfort, followed by an apparently empty facility, the wooden door and the aforementioned brilliant sunlight.

'Can I have a shower?' asked Ethan and Oliver practically at once.

'Of course you can.' You could tell Mum was not having to clean floors or do the washing up. She was so relaxed about everything. I practically gagged on my natural 'no way, it's not for you' response. I'm much happier with the laissez faire approach but I know my role is to be the hard man of the duo. The brothers then had a fight about who would go first, of course, but it was resolved amicably for once and two happy boys went off to the bathroom to get wet and warm and immerse themselves in hospital towels.

When you first acquire a disabled child I think it is inevitable that you get tied up with all the different aspects of their condition. I have vague memories at this point of the 'problems' conversation. I am pretty sure that we sat round that tiny dish containing our new son and discussed the seemingly endless list of potential medical conditions. Heart, blood, bowel, joints all had to be tested. It seemed that every part of his body could and would be affected by that extra chromosome and every part therefore had to be measured and assessed.

What intrigues me at this distance is how little of that conversation I can remember. I have vague recollections of him going off for tests, of white coated nurses coming in and jabbing his heels on a regular basis (it made me wince every time), of clipboards and charts and numbers and graphs. But it is only vague. It is almost as if it did not really matter. As if what really counted was that he was there and he was ours.

I have a favourite photograph from that time. In it our three older children are pictured sitting on the edge of that hospital bed while across all three lies the recumbent form of Caleb. He's in that baby state of half awake, half asleep, almost as if he's only waiting for them to go away so he can get back to his sun-bed, but at the same time there is a palpable excitement about the photo. Here we have our new brother, they seem to be saying, and we're really proud of him. Looking at it I cannot believe how young they all look, and yet how knowing. Somehow they are all aware that this one is a little different. This one will need all of us to help him and we are all going to be there.

Anyone who has a disabled child will tell you that you get very used to being in hospital. Caleb was incredibly healthy, but even he seemed to spend vast amounts of time visiting various hospital buildings.

It began with that first stay. Our first child, Rachel, had been kept in for a few days, really only because she was a first child. With our second, Oliver, Alison had managed a great escape. She had practically abducted one of the doctors in order to get the right form signed so she could leave without staying the night. The doctor wasn't quite quivering after the experience but I could see that he was glad to let us go. As we left, the building should have collapsed around our fleeing legs, like one of those slo-mo film sequences, if the hospital had lived up to its billing. With our third, Ethan, there was no visit to the hospital, just a large plastic sheet to be disposed of and a living room to be sponged down (not really – it was all very hygienic). So for Alison to stay in for over a week was a shock to us all, though probably a good thing as it got us properly prepared for what was to come.

For some reason the most vivid memory from those endless hospital visits is probably our last trip to have his heart scanned. It was the last major visit and somehow summed up my experience. Firstly, Caleb was provided for in the best possible way. The waiting room walls were covered in beautifully painted murals, there were toys everywhere and the staff were delightful. I have a vague memory of someone actually employed to play with the children. This may be a false memory but it is quite strong – and what a fabulous idea. All around were children clearly far sicker than Caleb. The give-away nasal tubes, the wheelchairs, the shrunken faces or bodies all bore testimony to severe heart problems. However, what was always surprising was how un-shrunken were their parents. I remember no miserable faces, no tired eyes, no exhausted slumping. It may have been the innervation of being in a place where you were looked after, but I don't think so. I just think that, exhaustion and lack of sleep aside, these were people with hope. Not hope always for future health, but hope for future life, hope that tomorrow at least they will be able to enjoy being with their children.

Second, and I know this is unique probably to Caleb, the news was all positive. The hole in his heart had closed all of its own accord, even to the point where there was no need to have antibiotics if he ever had an operation. That's code for entirely normal by the way. If you have any heart obstruction, antibiotics are given as a preventative in case anything gets lodged in an abnormal heart.

Caleb really never had any significant medical problems. He was always healthy in mind, body and spirit, as his Dad had requested. Oh, except once – but we'll come to that later. The doctor invited us into his Aladdin's cave of a consulting room, covered as it was with fabulous child-friendly murals, and told us the good news. He was as pleased as we were, which also seemed to be a feature of our hospital experience. The kind of people who choose to work with children like Caleb really care. There is no other way to describe it. Now I'm sure all medical staff care, but this seemed different. He was not just treating a patient, he was supporting a family, and he loved it.

In order to get to this appointment, we had to drive. Now I lived and drove in London for a while, and parking was always interesting, especially after they introduced a residents parking scheme, whose main achievement seemed to be to keep away any residents' friends, or family, or flat-mates or pretty much anyone else. Anyway, compared to parking at the John Radcliffe Hospital, that was a doddle.

For those of you who do not spend much time visiting hospitals, parking may seem a minor difficulty. They do after all have car parks. At least that's what you would expect. However this hospital was in the middle of a building programme, similar to that of pretty much every hospital I went to during the final years of the last government. As they will all still be paying for it when I am in geriatric care, I am not quite sure it was such a good idea, even though I can now enjoy sparkly new buildings. Certainly at the time it was a pain in the proverbial. The car park was a building site and the building site was a car park. Wherever you went there seemed to be an equal measure of signs proclaiming that you had better watch out for if you park too long your car will be towed away and crushed, and signs welcoming you to this wonderful new world that the concrete mixers and earth movers were opening up. It was, at the very least, confusing. What was more confusing for me, a hospital virgin at the time, was that I was expected to pay more for my short-stay parking than I would be if I had been in for open heart surgery. I'm still not sure I understand the logic. Free at point of need – unless you bring a car. Then you'll have to hock your grandmother and sell your children for experimentation, as Monty Python would have it. I exaggerate of course, but even now it seems a bit odd to be charged fifteen quid to park on a bit of muddy grass so you can visit your disabled son and your post-pregnant wife or take your child for a potentially life-threatening examination. Well that's big society conservatism for you.

The one time we did not have to pay these exorbitant fees was one of the most rewarding and amusing visits. It spanned a lot of days and occurred when Caleb was about five. It had a wonderful name based on its initials, Hotpack or something, and everyone in the know talked about it as if you were utterly stupid not to know. You know the kind of thing,

'When's your Spyrack, then? Ours is next month.'

'Not 'til September? Isn't that a bit post-nasal?'

As usual, as a man, I felt lost amid all this certainty. Just call it something normal, like pre-school overview (which is roughly what it was), we want to cry. But then of course we'd get that look. Poor thing, he's not kept up again. Maybe we could find a good remedial class for him.

Now I know men do exactly the same thing. We replace everyday words with weird ones just to make ourselves feel more important. I think my least favourite is 'going forward' rather than 'in the future' or even 'next', but I have a pretty strong revulsion for 'I'm just giving you a 'heads up' on…' What's wrong with 'listen' – it worked for Jesus. I cannot see 'I'm just giving you a heads up on sowing which might help going forward' having quite the same impact, can you?

Anyway we went for the Toepack, or whatever, with happy hearts. We'd been told it would be a really positive experience, and we were looking forward to having a whole week focused on Caleb. That was until the psychologist started his examination. Caleb was in playful mood. This means causing trouble, or at least that's how it seems to the uninitiated. In the right frame of mind, he will just wander around randomly throwing stuff. When he was younger it used to be plates. We'd be sitting at the table having a normal meal. One of us would be helping Caleb, when suddenly, in one brief moment of inattention, we'd turn back to find a plate full of food flying across the room. Pretty early on we moved to plastic plates as you can guess, but it was fairly messy even then. His favourite though was the cup trick. He'd drink some of the juice and then, to show he had had enough, or just for an effect, he would turn the cup upside down on the table. The resultant Niagara of juice usually managed to soak a few pairs of trousers.

So, Caleb had had enough of tests and the psychologist had a test that would make any child weep with frustration. Black line drawings of the dullest and most obscure objects were paraded in front of Caleb, while he was expected to match them to a relevant, and similarly tedious, picture. My two favourites were the drawing of an old style telephone with a rotary dial, which of course he'd never seen, and a drawing of the globe, which was so outside his orbit it might as well have been Jupiter. He decided that it was a game of catch. He did the throwing and the examiner had to catch. Bless the man, he just got on with it as if nothing had happened. Of course this was the worst possible response. The less he took note, the more ambitious were Caleb's attempts to get a rise out of him. 'It's a game silly, why won't you play?' he seemed to be saying. Cards began to fly around the room, while his parents quietly bounced their heads against the walls. Needless to say, Caleb did not score very highly, and his parents were in dudgeon.

'Why did he behave that way?' we meant the psychologist of course, we almost cried at each other. 'Caleb's much brighter than that.' 'What were those stupid pictures for? That's not a fair test.' And then we got it. The worse the result the better for Caleb. So what if Caleb came out as slower than a frog and dafter than a monkey. We knew better. And ever after every organisation that ever had to assess him for support, financial and otherwise, would have that test to guide them. Caleb needs everything you've got, it would shout. Did the psychologist mean it that way? I've no idea, but we have been very grateful for that man. He taught us that apparent setbacks are often the moments when things are actually going in your favour.

The rest of the Tierack was pretty positive. We learnt that Caleb found fine motor skills difficult, and so was going to find writing really hard. Not only was he going to struggle with the idea of reading and writing words, but he was also going to find the mechanics of it difficult as well. This has certainly been true, though it is intriguing that he is also very delicate in the way he manipulates his cars and his trains. He will spend hours lining them up in meticulous order, first putting them down and then gently pushing them into place so that they fit perfectly. Sometimes he uses the windowsill. Then everything else is cast onto the floor first. Sometimes it's the top of his plastic garage. After they are lined up, they will be carefully pushed down the car slide so that they crash onto the floor. Sometimes he uses his little play table. Some are discarded, apparently randomly but actually after careful choice. These are thrown across the floor, while the select few are meticulously arranged so as to cover the table top.

He does the same with his animals. This is an assortment of creatures, mythical, pre-historical, farmyard, which inhabit a large plastic box. They have variously been bath toys, sandpit toys, farm toys and chew toys, but suddenly they became arranged toys. I returned from work one day to find them at the back of the lounge put in a perfect circle, all facing in. It was almost too beautiful to tidy away, and stayed there until another set of toys took its place. This happened about four times before the game became tired and he moved on to other pursuits.

At the end of a week of tests we received a report. It told us, though in more numerous and more complicated words, that Caleb was rubbish at just about everything, or at least that's how it felt to me. Our beautiful child was off the normal chart (at the bottom) for practically everything (except presumably throwing test cards across the room). They had special charts for children with Down's Syndrome, of course, where he featured quite well, but it did not somehow work for me. I did not love him any less, you mind, but it is easy to harbour vague hopes that he might be like that man with Down's Syndrome who learnt five languages and seven musical instruments. You retain a vague hope with a disabled child that they will be the exception that has few if any problems. Rather like that bizarre expectation people have that they will win the lottery, you know it is not something to bank on but it somehow sits at the back of your mind. Well, the Sitback (or whatever it's called) blew that away. Our Caleb was profoundly bad at lots of things that other children could do without even trying. I have to say that this was, also profoundly, releasing. No longer did we need to compete. There would be no expectation of success and every piece of progress however small could be celebrated.

If only we'd realised this sooner, I wonder if the rest of our children would be much happier. One of the things no one tells you loudly enough when you have a disabled child is to watch out for the effect on the other children. I am not revealing too much, I think, if I suggest that the lives of Caleb's siblings are at times a little troubled. I remember recently, after a particularly difficult argument about how to deal with one child's challenging behaviour suggesting (all too loudly, if I recall correctly) that if we would only treat him more like we do Caleb he might get better, because punishment sure wasn't working. After nearly twenty years teaching and four children, I have to reveal that I have no idea how a child's mind works. I vaguely suspect that being loved by your parents and liked by as many other people as possible is about all there is to it.

The other thing we came to realise after the tests was that Caleb is actually good at lots of things, and often the ones that really matter. He is excellent with people, for example, being able to transform a crying teenager with one cuddle, or set a whole room laughing just by putting his legs behind his head (while he is sitting eating at the table – they just appear from under the edge of the table, and stick straight up either side of his ears). He is also very good at running away.

My favourite story about his escapology involves a trip to a swimming pool party. Caleb gets invited to loads of parties, some of which are wonderfully odd for him. We are, for example, going bowling this week. This time it was a pool party. Caleb loves water. He has a float-coat, but prefers to stand just in his depth and drop under water for ages, almost as if he is trying to become a fish. However, he cannot swim at all. He just sinks, quietly, to the bottom.

Alison got to the party on time and went in to where the Mums were congregating. It was one of those odd pools where they think that a suitable atmosphere for a cup of coffee and a quiet read is the same atmosphere needed for splashing around in wet knickers. In this place, as usual, the coffee drinkers suffered in a tropical steam room while the swimmers shivered whenever they stopped to take a breath. As a result there was no real barrier between congregating mothers with young children and the sloping 'beach' that led to the pool, which intermittently produced huge crashing waves. At this point Alison realised that she had left Caleb's costume in the car, so she turned to one of the Mums,

'Would you mind keeping an eye on Caleb while I run back to the car?'

The reply, from this very conscientious friend, who knew Caleb well, was of course in the affirmative. Well it does not need me to draw a picture. When Alison returned seconds later Caleb was not in the immediate vicinity. He had shot through the railings and was currently enjoying the thundering waves crashing around his fully clothed lower half. I was not there to witness the next moments, but I can picture the horrified friend and my determined wife wading out to rescue him from the waters.

My other favourite escape story takes less time to tell. It merely involves us at home and serves to illustrate that it was not Alison's friend's fault that Caleb escaped. When Caleb first arrived home, I put a back gate on the garden and we have always been very careful to ensure that he cannot get out at the front of our house. There is a shallow stream just over the road and a play park beyond, where he was once found when someone had taken their eyes off him for a moment. Anyway this time, he was there in the lounge, and then he was gone. The front door was closed, the side gate was closed so he could not have got out, but nevertheless we searched everywhere. I went across the road to the play park. I search up and down the stream. I checked our neighbours to see if he had got in there but to no avail. I may even have thought of calling the police, as they have sometimes patrolled the woods near our house looking for lost children (One lost child actually, and I should point out that these woods are tiny and safe).

Anyway, he was nowhere to be found. Then came a cry from the house. 'I've found him.' If you've ever lost a child you'll know how that feels. It's pretty good I can tell you. But where was he? Well, he'd gone out into the back garden, seen that our neighbours had chickens in their garden and crawled under the fence to meet them. Simple you might think. Simple yes, but only Caleb would do it. Other children have a concept of boundaries. He does not. It keeps us on our toes. And in a sense that is where this leaves us – on our toes. While Caleb was in hospital he was safe, he was protected. Outside he is ours to keep safe, to protect, for he will not protect himself. This is his great strength, he has no boundaries to others. He does not take count of his affections and limit them. He just loves. But it is also the great demand on us, for we must patrol the borders, not to defend him from others or others from him, but just to protect him from danger. And it is a lifetime's commitment.

In The Bedroom

There is something strange about leaving hospital with a newborn baby. The baby has been in this bubble of protection for days. Everything has been tailored to every need. The temperature is kept at a constant 80°F, warm enough to melt lead it seems, but ideal for the minute bundle. Whenever food is needed, food is on tap. Nipples may crack, breast may bulge, but the dear little thing gets its four-hourly nourishment on the dot, timed by the clock.

The experience for Dad is rather similar. The temperature in the home, usually a steady 60°F can, in the absence of the avenging angel, be cranked up to the ideal 75°F. Food, usually healthy and nourishing, can be delivered warm and in its cardboard wrapping, the way nature intended. And not a bulging breast in sight!

It's only Mum who suffers. Or at least so she says. I can fully understand that early hardship. It is hard not to wince when you first spot a woman walking down the corridor with that strange bow-legged gait of the newly minted mother. And the first child does serious damage to nipples previously reserved for other purposes. But it cannot be that hard to lie around in a cosy room all day with the occasional visit to mind the hours. I, for one, can see some significant advantages. You could get on with the serious business of inspecting your toenails for those odd hard bits that accumulate when you're not watching. You could read the book that has sat beside the bed for months. You could have a rest, for pity's sake.

But no, women just want to get home. So there comes a day when the great move must take place. No amount of bribing with promises of a McDonald's McChicken Sandwich being brought to the bedside will have any effect, and the baby must now leave the hospital.

The first thing is to check everything is ready. Even buying the car seat was quite a trauma. It is just astonishing how much baby stuff costs. Now I know they've done some survey on the cost of bringing up children which prices it at a gazillion pounds, plus the rest if you go private for education (it would be cheaper to adopt a Panda). But it's rather different when you actually go into one of these Mother-Stuff shops. Not Father-Stuff, please note, we may (or may not) pay the bills, but it is the Mrs. who does the shopping. Apparently even for men's clothes, which I suppose should not surprise me. A leading internet shop only puts men's stuff on its website to get women looking at it when they are buying presents for their husbands. No men actually buy any of it.

So you walk into the Mother-Stuff shop, dutifully towed along, and faint at the prices. They are just extraordinary. And then you realise you're going to have to buy all of it. It's not like a clothes shop where if you're lucky you'll come out with a pair of trousers (which you can then take back three days later). In the Mother-Stuff shops you need one of everything and two or three of lots of it. You need an articulated lorry just to get it all home. In addition, none of it makes much sense. I know it's obvious to the old hands, but I always wonder how many different places to lie down a baby really needs. If the shops are to be believed it's at least six: a car seat, a buggy, a pram, a bouncy chair, a cot and a Moses basket. Some of them try to combine two of these, but you kind of know that will end in disaster. You'll be turning the car seat into a buggy, when your finger will get caught in the catch, you'll scream and wrench it away and the baby will come flying out because the space-age straps had not quite clicked together properly. Social services will ask why the baby has a broken nose, the wife will leave you because, surprise, surprise, she doesn't believe your explanation, you'll lose your home, be cast on the street and moulder away in the gutter for the rest of your life. And all because you were too stingy to buy separates.

So you've got all the kit. You've brought the car seat with you, as per instructions. At home all the other stuff is ready in a huge pile in the baby's newly painted room. The thermostat is up for once. Everything is in place. Only the new baby is needed to bring this sterile world into noisy, smelly life. But you are ignorant of all this, for this is your first baby. Unlike previous generations there is no eager mother-in-law waiting at home to help (thank God), and so no one has any real clue what to do. Of course, the woman of your life will assume authority and with good reason. Up to this point it is probable that every child you have ever held has struggled and screamed. And who can blame them. You probably picked it up gently, thinking that was the best way. This communicates 'valuable' to you, but screams 'incompetent' to the baby, 'this one will drop me – get away quick'.

We produced the first grandchild in my family, and I vividly remember her plopped in the middle of the floor at her first Christmas, while my brothers sat around staring. It was as if she was an alien artefact that had appeared in their midst. My younger brother, brave as always, tried to hold her, in a rather helpless manner. Sure enough she screamed, he blenched and passed her back like a ticking bomb. Now here we were in the same position, but this time it was ours and there was no one to whom we could pass her back. Help!

It was a beautiful spring day, the perfect Easter Sunday. She had been born on Good Friday, and named after the Easter lamb, so it was appropriate that she would leave her temporary 'tomb' on the third day. For us it was terrifying. Suddenly we were on our own with no one to ask what to do next. This was emphasised by my first attempts to put the car seat in the car. It reminds me of those first attempts to remove your partner's bra. The pressure to appear nonchalant, the total ignorance of how these bloody things work, the fumbling with random straps. There was no one but us in the car park, but it felt like an audience of millions was watching. In my imagination, all those other successful, confident, capable parents were looking on.

Once she was in the car, everything was ok. I drove with a serious degree of extra care, it must be noted, but we had made the move, taken the plunge, or whatever other dull metaphor you want to suggest. What I mean is that the moment of responsibility had arrived and we had accepted it. We'd done that nine months before, of course, when we'd left off the condom, but now it was for real. Rachel was coming home.

For some reason I have few memories of our babies in the house in their early days, except for those things happening in the bedroom. I do, of course, remember the endless array of grandparents and well-wishers, hoping to hold the baby, especially oddly enough with our second child. This is largely because it meant that I didn't get to hold him nearly enough, which saddens me even now, unfortunately. But it is in the bedroom that my strongest memories of those early days were formed.

When I had lived in London, I had met a curate whose children seemed to spend most mornings clustered in the family bed. It sounded awful to me. I like my space and I like my sleep, so the thought of a load of boisterous children bouncing into my face every morning filled me with horror. This was before my teaching days (and long before my parenting days) so children were a kind of freak show to me. It is hard to anticipate what you will feel when you have your own. But now I did I was fairly determined to get her trained early. No coming into my bed for her. For some reason Alison went along with this, and poor Rachel was shunted out into a slightly elderly Moses basket practically immediately.

Do not be too alarmed, please. We kept her right next to us alongside the bed and kept a close eye on her, practically all night. This nightly vigil was initially because it is hard to sleep when you first get a baby. You have this vague sense that they may just decide not to breathe. It's odd when you think about it. A few million years of evolution has meant that breathing is pretty natural to us humans, and it is unlikely that a couple of Johnny-come-latelys like us are going to be much help in keeping it going. There is the terror of cot death, of course, but it is clearly impossible to stay up all the time, so there is not much point in doing more than to stop smoking and put the baby to sleep on her back.

What we found out fairly early on is that the phrase 'sleeping like a baby' actually means waking up every couple of hours and screaming, thrashing around in your cot for about an hour before you wake up, and ensuring, as much as is in your power, to prevent anyone anywhere near from sleeping at all. Every morning, or what passed for morning during those early days, she used to kick with her legs and throw her arms around for ages before she actually woke up. We used to say that she was 'swimming for England'. It's not funny I know, but when you are severely sleep deprived anything is worth doing that will lighten the mood a little.

This seemed to go on for ever and then, after four weeks, she slept for four hours and I walked into work as if I was walking on air. The birds sang, the sun shone and even the unwashed faces of the first class of the day looked angelic in my eyes. I had slept and the world was wonderful.

After six weeks, we expelled her to her own room. I would say that we slept better, but it is doubtful. Alison had this quaint notion that feeding the baby was a shared experience and used her sharp elbows to wake me so I could join in. 'If I was meant to feed her, God would have given me breasts,' I wanted to shout, but when you're lying comatose next to a woman starved of sleep, low on blood sugar and mildly post-natal you do not make any false moves. Who knows if she slept with something sharper than an elbow under her pillow? I for one was not going to risk finding out.

When Rachel moved out things were a little better for me to start with as I usually sleep through nightly noise. However, it quickly became clear that though, bless her, Alison would do the feeding, shivering under a thin blanket, I was on duty for getting the baby back to sleep. This was not as bad as it seems, as we had that bizarre heating system called night storage. For some incomprehensible reason this meant that the house was pretty warm at three o'clock in the morning, when you were usually wrapped up warm in bed, even though it was freezing at six o'clock in the evening, when you wanted to sit quietly with a book. At least it meant that I did not shiver, as I sat with my perfect little bundle for hour after hour. We truly communed together, usually on her bedroom window seat, as she stubbornly resisted the return to slumber.

Oliver, poor thing, got an even rougher ride. We were tough by then and he got booted out after about 2 weeks. He was also less demanding and so received fewer of those magic midnight cuddles than had Rachel. I sometimes think that I've been playing catch up with him ever since. Beware the second child, I want to say to other families, especially if there's a third, for they will not get enough of your time and nothing later will make up for it.

Oliver's appearance had been at a particularly challenging time. Rachel was still very young, I had just moved jobs and we had all, therefore, moved home. Alison had not really recovered from feeding Rachel before Oliver was conceived. It had even snowed heavily – our first snow for many years. More than all that though, the in-laws had taken up residence. They came to help at the birth (well not actually at it, of course) and had stayed on for Christmas, which was weeks later. We love them dearly, but, like all the best in-laws, they feel that they are there to help, whereas we wanted them to get out and have fun without us.

Ethan in contrast had a much easier time. He appeared at home with blessed rapidity, and at an ideal time, so that he could be washed, dried, fed and put to bed by about 11 in the evening, just as we were going to bed. Somehow this serendipity softened us so as to allow him, on his first night out in the world, to share our bed with us. In the morning the two older children came in.

'Do you notice anything different?' asked Alison.

New pillowcases, new pyjamas, even 'you've washed your hair' (cheek) were trotted out, but only when Alison pulled back the cover to reveal the still sleeping baby, did the penny drop. They were, I am glad to say, pleased, though somewhat surprised, to see Ethan's still sleeping form. We had been rather more pleased and really quite astonished that he had allowed us six hours sleep. It was a revelation: babies that sleep through do arrive in the world. Thereafter Ethan has always remained the easy one. As a result we were very unprepared for Caleb.

How can I best explain this? I think it is to tell you about today. Today Caleb slept through. We were home late on Sunday and he woke late on Monday. Today Tuesday he woke late again. Late is after 7 if that means anything to you. He is 7, so I suppose it is appropriate. That means that for the last seven and a half years Caleb has been waking us up in the night. Not every night, I should admit, but it is common to the point where we notice if he sleeps through rather than the other way round.

This is not unusual for children with Down's Syndrome. Someone of our acquaintance has two children, both with Down's Syndrome. One of them is also autistic, which is a very common additional difficulty for children with Down's Syndrome, and almost always gets up in the night and wanders around the house. He is older than Caleb. Now, because we knew this, we used to have a gate on Caleb's room. For many years it was a child's safety gate, such as you might commonly use to stop young children climbing the stairs. Unfortunately he learned to climb it, so one day he appeared in our room, with a mischievous grin on his face.

We replaced it with a dog gate. I saw one in a neighbour's house and it seemed an obvious solution. It did seem a little odd buying a dangerous dog gate for your son, and we had vague thoughts that social services might come and take us away in a padded van as a result, so we did not exactly advertise it. But it worked. He stayed in his room and we slept. That is until he found an escape solution. This cunning plan involved one of the most fearsome weapons in his arsenal. We are not speaking here of fingernails, though they are incredibly destructive, but of something far more damaging in its effect and impossible to guard against. We are of course talking bodily fluids (and other things less fluid). He had reached the age when he could control his excretions, and so had no excuse, but woe betide us if we left him in his room too long. It wasn't quite the Nile running under the door, but he could have won prizes with his wee patch. Bless him, he at least had the sense to get out of bed, but I think he was just making a point.

'I'm going to squat by this gate and do my stuff,' he seemed to be saying, 'and there's nothing you can do about it.' That was just about ok. That is until he used his more potent weapon. When that toilet smell wafts through the house, it may easily be blamed on small boys leaving the bathroom door open, and that is the parents' hope. But not this time. Caleb had made his mark in no uncertain terms. 'I want out,' was the message, and we got it loud and clear. So the gate was removed - and so was sleep. At least until the next solution could be found.

There is another aspect to regular night disturbance that it seems to me I should touch on. Sex. Or lack of it. Alison, if she ever reads this, will be instantly groaning. 'Does he ever think about anything else?' The answer is, of course, of course not. Now I have various theories about sex, which I will not bore you with, but let's note that having little sleep is bad for sex on lots of fronts. First the 'too tired' excuse is valid, as are most of the others. You see, whatever anyone tells you, having a disabled child is hugely demanding. It affects us all differently, of course. Some moan, some get depressed, some cope, some develop stress-related illness. Oh and me? I'm just grumpy. It is hardly likely there will be much frolicking between the sheets under those circumstances.

And, even if you weren't too tired, and I'm not sure I ever am, there's a decent chance of being interrupted. Now I know all those marvellous sex counsellors are saying to get a lock on the door, but it's not that easy. By the time you've got up, put the lock on and got down again, the moment has probably passed. And anyway, someone banging on your door is not a great deal better than someone standing at the bottom of the bed saying, 'what are you doing to Mummy?'. 'Just rolling over to look at the alarm clock, darling' cons no one. No, having a disabled child is a wonderful contraceptive and without all the bother of contraception.

There are of course some compensations. Now not having to have sex is not one of them – your husbands and wives need you. Otherwise they will feel neglected, and with good reason. But having Caleb appear at odd hours of the morning is sometimes quite beautiful.

'In bed, now, pease' were the first words I heard this morning. Our usual reply is 'no pees, no carrots and no broccoli' which he loves. 'No carrots, no broccoli, just pease.' I'm really not sure how much of it he does on purpose, but his versions of words are all wonderful. I'm sure all families have them. We have 'radurators' rather than radiators because that's how Rachel first said it. The great thing about Caleb is that this mispronunciation has been going on for years so there are even more of them.

I remember one morning he came into bed and started talking avidly about 'Nace'. Alison was out somewhere, possibly getting breakfast from the local Waitrose, and I was left on my own to translate this mysterious word. I cannot remember how long it was but, after what seemed like forever, I sussed that he was talking about trains. 'Thomas' was fairly clear and we knew that 'Peter Wham' was Peter Sam. It wasn't until I translated 'Car-oh-y' as Skarloey that I got it. 'Ah, Rheneas.' 'Yes,' he replied, 'Nace.' He still says 'Nace' two years later, along with 'suttup' (taught him by my oldest son), 'divideee', 'otchin' and 'tains'. On the other hand, many other words have become increasingly clear, with occasional whole perfect sentences. These are always concrete, like 'read book now' and often refer to television. He rather engagingly does not often ask for something but simply states that it is permitted, so that 'may I watch?' is 'allowed 'otchin' NOW', which is actually far more persuasive. Maybe I should try it, 'Allowed sex, NOW.'

The real reason we find ourselves so often in the same bed as him is that he loves company. It is not unusual to find one of us scrunched up next to him, evening, nighttime or morning, in his shrunken child's bed. He just loves to stick his feet down between your bent legs. This is fine except that every so often he will pull them out again, scrapping his toenails on your sensitive thighs (or other more sensitive parts) on the way up. It's kind of cosy but not exactly comfortable.

When he was young he would lie next to you and play with your fingers. It was a sort of endless game of tag with just a few slow-moving fingers as bate. He'd touch them and then roll them away to be touched again. It was surprisingly and inexpressibly beautiful and intimate. Those days are largely over now though he will still fiddle with anything he can get his hands on. This means that, on those rare occasions when we find him in bed in the morning, his hands will usually be invisible in his trousers. Typical boy, I hear you cry, and quite right too. Why not? It's soft and squidgy and comforting. Oh and always ready to hand, of course, and ready warmed so far better than a cuddly toy will ever be.

This fiddling is fine if it is part of drifting off quietly to sleep. Unfortunately sometimes it is rather the opposite. On one occasion, I was left to look after the children while Alison went off to visit her family or something. At four o'clock in the morning Caleb awoke. Being a little lazy, and noticeably naïve, I thought I'd bring him into bed with me, so we could both have a bit of company. What a mistake. First he started fiddling with my ears. That was just about bearable but then he started trying to see how far his fingers could reach up my nose. A long way is the answer, I can tell you. I thought that they would come out the top of my head. He'd have got a job with an Egyptian embalmer.

Now of course it became a game. My thrashings became more vigorous the more pain he induced so he tried the next level of agony. If a nose produced a struggling father, could sticking his fingers in my eyes produce an even greater reaction. The answer was in the affirmative. It is surprising how difficult it is to screw up your eyes against a persistent fingernail. Somehow there's always a way in. Well that was it. He was expelled back to his own bed, and I was left to staunch a mildly bleeding nose and check whether I could still see out of both eyes. It meant I had to sit out of my warm bed on a draughty landing to check he went to sleep, but better that one of us slept than neither of us.

And that's it really. At the last, bed is for sleeping. If only children worked that out a bit sooner we'd all be happy.

Growing

Delayed. When it flickers onto the electronic board it sends chills down the spine of the unsuspecting traveller. Delayed. How long must I stay here? Will it be hours? Or days even? The sense of uncertainty turns simple anxiety into deep desperation. No plans can be made. No provisions can be bought. If I leave my seat the train may come while I'm away and then when will I ever get home. 'We apologise for the delay. This is due to a breakdown on the line.' The simple announcement contains nothing to halt the spreading dread. A train rushes past on the neighbouring line. A sense of anticipation rises beginning somewhere in the stomach and finally lifting the chest with hope. But then, nothing. Delayed. Still, delayed.

Everyone has a story of being stuck somewhere uncomfortable. My favourite involves a simple journey from Sheffield to York. I had to take four trains, each of which was carefully timed to connect and so smooth me through my journey. It was a day off work and I had plans to read a paper, have a leisurely cup of coffee, surreptitiously pick my nose, all those sweet pleasures of a single man's private journey. Instead it was an exercise in angst. The first train was delayed, so I missed the first connection. The second train was delayed so I arrived at my destination too late for the quiet coffee, too late to buy, let alone read, the paper. I did not even get round to any satisfying picking as I spent the whole time in that on-the-dirty-loo position so favoured by the anxious commuter, desperate to exit the train at full throttle and so shade a few seconds off my time. On the way back I had less to miss and, glory of glories, one of the trains was on time. But then, as if the excitement was too much, the last connection went disastrously wrong, and I was home just in time to check if the children still recognised me and slobber on the wife.

Delayed. When you first start investigating what will happen to your child with Down's Syndrome as they grow, the word is offered as a kind of easy way in. 'Your son will be about 50% delayed in their educational development.' It is probably meant to sound comforting. A neat handle on things. 'All my other children talked at 18 months, and he's 3 and still not talking. Oh that's all right, he's 50% delayed.' Hmm. 'All my other children learned to use the toilet by 2, and he's 5 and still spreading his faeces all over the living room carpet. That's OK, he's 50% delayed.' Pardon. 'All my other children were sleeping through by 2, and he's 8 and still gets up in the night, goes downstairs, takes the chocolate spread out of the cupboard and starts spooning it into his mouth.' Ugh! It just may be that the label is less comforting than it seems.

I have my own theory. It was developed in the crucible of constipation. Anyone with a child with Down's Syndrome will recognise the scenario. It's been four days and they haven't been to the loo. Oh yes, they have peed all right, but no poo. All that happens is the stomach gets a bit firmer and starts to bulge in unexpected places. Eventually you know that you have to get advice. And the reply is simple – just scoop it out. Needless to say it was one of those jobs ideally suited to the gentler sex. I put out the rubbish, cut the firewood, put up shelves and, that most physically demanding of all jobs, drive the car. That leaves you, dear, to spoon the poo out of your two-year-old son's bottom. I don't think I was even in the house. 'Just got an urgent 'phone call from the office, love, must go!' Anyway, on analysis as to why he might get so bizarrely stuck up, we found out that his tubes are all a bit narrower. Now, I realise that this is not very technical – I am sure the medics have long words for the phenomenon – but it set me thinking. What if all his tubes are narrower? The tubes in his brain would pass electric impulses more slowly. The tubes that make up his tendons would, like thinner elastic bands, flex more fully. He would have more tubes in his muscles, so he would actually be stronger, which explains a lot. It is probably nonsense, but I offer it here as an alternative to 50%. 'He's got narrow tubes.' Oh well, maybe not. But it helped me.

I sit and watch the grainy video footage of Caleb's first hesitant steps. He has one of those baby walker things and is pushing it pell-mell across our living room floor, caring not a jot what or who he bumps into, just thrilled with the speed of locomotion. Out of shot the siblings are egging him on with inarticulate cries of encouragement and an occasional raucous burst of giggling as he crashes into sofa or wall. Caleb doesn't mind – he's just so thrilled to be up and active. However, his stance is something to behold.

Humour me for a minute and try the Caleb shuffle. Imagine that your hips have become temporarily glued, possibly with that old-fashioned grey-green gunge that never seems to quite harden until weeks later when you come back to find it has oozed everywhere and is impregnably tough. Now let every other part of your body go floppy. Arms are not carefully bent at the elbow, but languidly dangling from the shoulders. The torso is not rigid and upright but rolls from side to side, from front to back, as if the angle of attack is driving the motion rather than any deliberate policy on behalf of the motivator. Now imagine that on your feet someone has strapped the heaviest, clumpiest, meanest boots possible. They are two sizes too big on the outside, and cause the legs to swing wildly whichever way they are first set in motion. Now run. Run like you're winning a race and any loss of effort will mean the devastation of coming second. Run like your very life depends on it, but remember that this fact makes the whole thing more exciting rather than more frightening. Now you are running like Caleb. And it is beautiful to watch.

Surprising amounts of time can be spent just watching Caleb move. He has this delicate pincer movement with his fingers, as if he is modelling himself on Lady Bracknell drinking tea. When moving anywhere he seems to be placing his feet as if crossing a waterbed, or a floating pontoon. And when he climbs, the limbs take up quite impossible angles, reaching not just up to his face, like some champion sports climber, but right above. Prima ballerinas could take lessons.

We once had a leg lifting competition at the dining room table. Caleb started so as to show us how it was done and effortlessly lifted both legs and wrapped them behind his head. Rachel was next in line and gamely attempted to imitate this extraordinary feat. Her dance training gave her limited advantage over those who were to follow and her legs duly made contact with her head, just. Ethan unsurprisingly got the most marks for noises. Squeals and grunts accompanied his efforts, which were dramatic, though not hugely successful. Mum came next with a worthy attempt, managing to get one leg somewhere near her earhole, but at the cost of some potentially serious work later with a physiotherapist. Oliver declined to join in at first, on the grounds that he was not going to win, and so, by definition, it was a stupid game. This left Dad. I dutifully took my best shot, as it were, though I rather hoped my tendons did not go bang, and forced my legs to go up in the air, vaguely in the direction of the ceiling. Oliver at last realised that there was no chance of coming last, and that allowing Caleb to win was an acceptable family policy, and came up with a brave imitation of a woman giving birth, legs up, mouth open, eyes wide in pain, but determined to get it done, and done now.

This legendary flexibility is a common source of family amusement. Only this morning Caleb demonstrated his absurd acrobatic talent. As he was eating his favourite chocolate spread bread, a small piece liberally covered with a large dollop of brown goo fell down and stuck to his heel. Most of us would either reach down and wipe it off, or quietly pretend it had not happened and scrape it against a chair leg. Caleb found a different method of dealing with the problem. He calmly lifted his leg to a point next to his mouth, turned his foot around with one hand and sucked it directly from his naked heel. It would be going too far to suggest there was rapturous applause, but certainly the assembled audience at the table were in some degree of awe. I expect Ethan asked, 'How does he do that?' as it seems to be almost his only question, but the rest of us just sat in stunned silence. It was hard to see Down's Syndrome as a disability when it provided a party trick such as that.

Caleb's flexibility is one thing that does not seem to have changed, from that first moment when the doctor on call held him out, balanced over her palm and showed us one sign of his condition, with the words, 'Look, he's floppy.' He looked more like something the butcher might offer for Sunday lunch than a new born child, a sort of plumb bag of bones and muscle, but thereafter it became a sign of Caleb as talented hero. 'Look at what my brother can do,' they would cry, as they wrapped his legs around his head a couple of times. And it's something that does not seem to change. However much better he gets at balancing, running, climbing or fighting, he will always be insanely bendy.

Other things, though, have changed a lot. When you first receive a child with that odd label, disabled, you wonder what he will be able to do. It always seems to focus on limitations. Will he walk? Will he speak? Will he add up? Will he read? Will he ever, ever leave home? For Caleb the answers have all been yes, even to the last question, though I'll believe it when I see it. This morning he was spelling out a two-syllable word. Was it 'bigger'? I can't remember. But I can remember that it was a triumph. As he gets older he falls steadily further and further behind his classmates, but no-one really notices, because every step forward is hard won, and so every step forward is a success to be treasured. It is as if time has slowed down enabling each moment to be savoured fully. In contrast to the normal rush of growing up where if you go away for a week you miss a vital moment of change, Caleb's moments of change are stretched out to months, years even, and there is almost no chance of missing them. When it takes four years to potty train, you certainly relish the moments of progress, though it would be lovely one day to stop having to wipe his backside for him.

It is interesting to wonder which of these two scenarios is the place for character. The old-fashioned approach to character of Rousseau and the like, suggests that it is something we create out of nothing. Bringing up a child is like painting on a blank canvass. You can tell from this that Rousseau knew bugger all about children. On his part it seems to have been deliberate, as he seems to have shipped all his off to the local orphanage as soon as he could get rid of them. But in his followers it is rather less forgivable. Anyone who has actually been a parent will be crying, nay screaming, 'If only...' or possibly, 'As if...' I have spent my life with children and young people and I have seen change of behaviour, development of intellect, flourishing of talent, but never change of character. My own are a case in point. They come out (in our case fly out), look at you and you think, 'Help, he's going to be trouble.' It's instant and, seemingly unfortunately in some cases, unchanging. However I'm very glad. I would not want the responsibility of creating character. It is enough to try and foster confidence, build resilience, enable individuality and control destructive urges, (all of which I've been useless at, by the way), without being responsible for the essence of who they are. And in case you're wondering, Caleb is definitely trouble.

As many have pointed out, far more eloquently than I, this character presents an emotional challenge for parents of children with Caleb's condition. Part of what makes Caleb, well, Caleb, is his Down's Syndrome. If he had been born with different genes, with only two copies of chromosome 21, he would not be Caleb. Or at least I suppose he'd be Caleb, because that is probably what we would have named him, but he wouldn't be the Caleb we know. Thus when people come along and talk about 'cures' for Down's Syndrome, as was recently suggested in a piece of American research, we find our feelings rather mixed. We would not have Caleb any different, but we would love him to be insulated from all the extra difficulties he may face. From limited life expectancy, from the despising jeers he will receive in place of the loving hugs as he moves from childhood to adulthood, from an inability to earn a living in this world of discrimination, from all this we would love him to be released. But then the realisation strikes. He would not be Caleb, and all that means in loss to all the world, including those who cannot cope with difference. His unique and powerful place in the world would not be filled. It may be only for a short time, but it is often those shorter lives that leave the greatest mark.

We recently had the privilege of attending a funeral. I know that sounds odd, but it was a privilege. She was severely disabled. She was very young. And she was inestimably beautiful. Her short and troubled life had more of an impact than many long and easy ones. The church was full to bursting. Every eye was full to flooding. And no one will ever forget her parents' courage in standing to speak of the beauty that shone in suffering. Few will know such a funeral, and very few will know how that strange bittersweet revelation of joy and sorrow can come at once. Until you sit in the quiet spot in the midst of the blaze can you ever know real peace. This is what we are offered as parents of the disabled. Let none try to take it away.

It is precisely the desire of many to take it away. The recent new non-invasive test for Down's Syndrome was heralded as a cure for the condition, when of course it was no such thing. Just as many children with Down's Syndrome will be conceived. It is just that even fewer of them will be allowed to grace this world with the healthy and beautiful ones who are permitted that strange chance. I have always found it ironic that the more we strive to populate our planet with the perfect and the wanted, the more those flawless children become a dangerous threat to the happiness of their parents. These perfect children often roam the streets causing havoc and misery wherever they go. If only they had a disabled brother at home they might have known what it meant to care and take responsibility. They might know that weakness was not something to fear and avoid, but an opportunity to love and to embrace. Or, to put it in my preferred way, 'Everyone needs a Caleb.'

Teachers can be so lovely. Caleb was in a group of four at school today doing Maths, and his teacher told his mother that he got some of the questions right more quickly than the others. My instant response was, as you can guess, 'I bet it wasn't the question: what is two plus two.' To which my dear wife retorted that it was more likely to have been, 'When is Christmas?' Nevertheless, while parents are taught to expect delay, it is rather neat that it is not 50%. He is ahead of most of his peers in socialisation, is pretty good with finding videos on 'you-tupe' and can get daddy to provide a 'puter with unwavering determination. Oh, and he can ride a horse.

Nothing really prepares you for the generosity of some of those with whom you come into contact. Nowhere is this more true than at Riding for the Disabled. Previously patronised by Princess Margaret (who else, as she was in spirit a horse), it is run by the most extraordinary horsy people, who give so much time and devotion it is heart-warming. Even more heart warming is the age profile. My eight year old is often led around the ring by someone whom you'd expect to see gracing the shopping precinct with a Zimmer frame on Saturday mornings. But here she is giving time, energy and the very few remaining years of her life to care for the cheeky and uncooperative child atop the mountain of horse next to her. I often wonder what would happen if the animal decided not to play ball. I think Caleb would be all right. He'd cling on and laugh. But I imagine the dear old ladies being flung around like one of my daughter's abused Barbie's – all spindly legs and disjointed arms rotating at strange angles (though not the bizarrely pert breasts, of course).

That's one week. The next week Caleb is being led round the school on a horse that he insists on calling Charlie (whatever its real name) by a child. She looks to be ten. Her limbs are matchstick thin. And the only hint that she's one of those tough horsey chicks is her pair of riding boots. Mum, who runs the session, has brought along her two daughters to help. And the youngest seems to be barely out of nappies. But then you see her face and you know that there will be no messing with this one. Horse watch out. Built like a stick insect she may be, but skinny elbows are unspeakably sharp. Behave. Or else.

The major sign of Caleb's improving riding skills is the number of helpers. First he needed three – one on each side and one leading. Then it was two – one on one side and one leading. This arrangement always struck me as quirky. What if what went wrong happened on the other side? Was Granny meant to vault the horse and catch Caleb as he fell down? Sure enough one day Caleb was particularly unwilling to join the fun and got down half way round. That's a big no-no as you might guess, and surprisingly dangerous. This is half a ton of semi-domesticated animal he is mixing with, and could result in serious injury. Unsurprisingly there was no ninja granny, just a severe teacher who appeared and hoicked little Caleb out of the melee. He seems to have got the message, as we have had no repeat and now he just has one leader. This one is surprisingly normal in age, a university student, bright (very – Cambridge) and articulate, who just seems to adore him. Another sign of development. He teases her mercilessly and she loves it, bless her. But who wouldn't?

In 1859, three world-changing literary works are published. Charles Dickens writes the final instalment of A Tale of Two Cities, Charles Darwin finally allows On The Origin of Species to go to press, and the first rulebook of Aussie Rules Football is produced. I confess to only having read one of these, but at least many would claim it was the most important. No it is not the Aussie rulebook, though I confess to a strange fascination with a game that appears to take the rugby concept to its proper end – unfettered violence. It is rather that oddly brief and strangely written work that began the unbridled gallop of the Theory of Evolution through the midst of our western culture. It is hard to think of any part of western thought that is unaffected by its simple but profound conclusions. The immense variety of life that we perceive on earth did not arise ready formed from some kind of prepubescent ooze, but as a result of historical contingency, of chance changes, forced into place by pressures from the natural environment. No longer did we need a god to snap his fingers (or roll some poo, in one case) so that life could arise out of nothing. Life just arose all by itself as the infinitely variable genetic code sought precedence over the dramatically changing world through which it drifted.

It is wrong to think that this immediately caused Christian clerics to foam at the mouth and start calling down fire from heaven to burn up all extant copies. Most Christians were unfazed, largely because they'd always rather felt that the text wasn't meant to be read scientifically anyway. Indeed it was more likely that secular authorities would treat ancient descriptions of the beginning of the world literally than religious ones. Napoleon even financed an expedition to Egypt in order to discover and read such texts for this very purpose, and he could hardly be called a stalwart of the Christian church. Darwin himself saw no conflict with faith, though whether this was to prevent the aforesaid book burning who can be sure. To my mind that is a very unlikely explanation as his bravery in declaring his own loss of faith in such a faith-filled culture hardly suggests a cowardly man where such things are concerned. It was suffering, in particular that of his daughter, that did for his beliefs, not evolution.

Indeed in the context of the time, the theory chimed rather well with some powerful theological ideas. The Hegelian concept of historical improvement, of social progress through contrasting ideas towards some ideal spirituality underlay much western thinking. Things were getting better and better, and mankind, already the pinnacle of creation, was growing and improving not just socially but also culturally. Now on top of all that we were progressing genetically as well. Man (and it was largely man, of course) was growing up.

This was all put paid to by the two wars with Germany. WWI reminded us that all our progress in technology just meant we were better at slaughtering each other. Now we could not only mass-produce cars, but we could mass-produce death as well, and on an industrial scale. WWII let us look deep into the heart of this human being and find that underneath all the progress and improvement lay the same old Adam, ready to torture and murder our fellow man, just for being different. Worse than that for evolution, the survival of the fittest became the destruction of the weakest. The accidental improvement of the human race through natural forces, became the deliberate refinement of one ideal kind of human through the eradication of any who did not quite fit. Evolution was employed by the Nazis to justify their murderous campaign and so became repulsive to those who opposed them.

Unfortunately, rather than recognising that evolution was not the Ascent of Man but rather the Divergence of Nature, some decided that the whole theory must be wrong, and that we had to go back to a previous certainty about God's creation of the universe. It did not worry the proponents of this idea that God had not been seen in quite this way in the past, so it was not exactly going back. What mattered was clarity in opposition to the ungodly theory known as evolution.

On one level they were right of course. As we have fewer genes than a grain of rice (less than half it seems), it is stretching things a little far to suggest that in evolutionary terms we are the pinnacle of natural selection, as if there were some single line of improvement with us at its end. Historical progress is a nineteenth century myth that suited those times and needs to be got rid of in these. In my view Creationists are right to assert the *creativeness* of God. If evolution actually meant giving up the idea of a creator God, as some today suggest, then the only response might well be to demonstrate that it is simply wrong. However, it does not. To claim that God made the world in six days is to assert scientific nonsense. But it is equally nonsense to claim that the study of the structures of a physical world can remove the reality of a spiritual creator. God is rather bigger than biology, good or bad.

But the best news is that evolution may be ultimately on the side of the concept of a creator God. For not only is evolution about divergence, about the continual and bountiful development of variety in living organisms. It is also about convergence, about the apparently unrelated development of similar structures, cultures and expressions between members of this extraordinary variety. It seems that many of us creatures sing songs - birds, whales, humans and more. It is almost as if the pattern of intelligent life is already written into the universe and all we are doing is discovering it. We are not, of course, descended from apes (though we might share a mutual ancestor) – we are, by contrast, quietly ascending to the heavens. Not getting better, but reaching towards a perfect pattern set out in the universal creation of all, seen and unseen.

What, you might well ask, has this got to do with Caleb? Well, I guess it is this. Watching Caleb grow is not about watching improvement. Yes, he can get better at doing certain tasks, at achieving certain functional goals, but this is not actually progress. What we must look for is the eternal song that his life is singing. Listen for that perfect pattern to which his life is always an imperfect approximation, but which can be discerned just on the edge of hearing. And, furthermore, it is a pattern that began long before he appeared. It is, if you like, written on the palm of God's hand, or, if you don't like, it is written in the convergent evolutionary character of all life, most fully expressed in human life. It is the song we all sing, out of tune, out of harmony, out of time, yet, once mixed with the angels', perfectly discerned by our creator. But it began not only for us as a whole but also for him as a one, long before birth. It begins for every womb-dweller as soon as they become human, as soon as that new individual is formed. What we do when we cut off that life is take away that voice, take one note of harmony out of the song. It may return in heaven but for now it is a loss of inexpressible sadness.

Learning

I have before me two of Caleb's Home Links books. They are common little exercise books which get filled in by his support staff every day to keep us up-to-date with his education. I acquired them from Alison just as she was about to throw them away because I thought they might contain some undiscovered gems of insight into Caleb's education. Alison, in a slightly dreary tone, warned me that they might be a little bit dull, but this did not adequately prepare me for the abject dreariness of everyday learning. Here's just one entry:

Painting. Encouraging Caleb to paint lines "car" – careful painting

½ apple at break.

Lots of yawning after break.

Counting out objects 1-5 and matching

correct number to objects, 1

Toilet before lunch.

Now I am sure each entry represents a whole plethora of delightful and careful teacher-student communication, but how can this represent a whole morning? I'll tell you how.

Most learning is extraordinarily dull. Yes, I know we teachers are meant to inspire and illuminate young minds with the wisdom of the ages, but I'll let you into a secret. Most learning is repetitive and dull. I don't necessarily mean it looks dull on the outside. Modern education has at its fingertips the most wonderful array of lively and inventive resources. I use internet, video, image, debate, discourse, dialogue and I'm not even very good at it. What I mean is that the actual learning bit is largely about doing the same thing over and over again. The trick is often to make it look like you're doing something different when really you're not. Some great teachers don't even do that. They engage the class with the force of their personality and everyone loves it.

This simple fact about education was revealed to me most clearly when my children started to do something that looked vaguely like mathematics. Now I don't know if you old lags remember starting proper maths. I do. I had the most fearsome of teachers. Her name somehow escapes me just now (hardly surprising as I routinely call my children by the wrong name) but her physique does not. She was built with the most enormous bosom (or bu-zoom, as my Gran called it). It was so large that if you got up close you could not see her face. She used to play the piano in a rather plinky-plonky way in assembly and I dimly remember her breasts extending so far as to hide the keys entirely, which might explain her playing, I suppose. Anyway to a young child this was terrifying. Was it the fear of getting lost under them and never coming out? Or was it simply the sense of an unstoppable gravitational field that would suck you into its orbit, so that you plunged to your death against a rocky (or in this case blubbery) planet?

Certainly when Mrs Huge (or something like that) spoke we listened in a hushed awe, as if she were officiating at some holy rite. But as we were the remedial class, what she mostly said seemed to be the equivalent of 'two twos are four'. I may misremember those early days of school, but I don't think so. Every day seemed to be learning tables, that is times tables, by rote. We would chant incessantly until our throats were dry and our minds blank apart from the repetitive sounds.

And I still hear them. Not her voice, but my own, chanting, 'Six sevens are forty-two'. It is automatic and unthinking. Now, in contrast, my children, brought up with progressive learning, have never had the equivalent of Mrs Hughes. They have never learnt their tables, and, largely as a result, they are bollocks at sums.

Education at its best is repetitive and dull. Sorry but there you are.

My favourite entries in Caleb's link book are those written by my dear wife. She tries to break from the norm and make them interesting. One reads, 'Went to watch Daddy run in the Oxford Town and Gown 10k' and later, 'Went with Daddy on trampoline'. What Daddy thought of gasping his way around central Oxford all morning and then being jumped on by his large son in the afternoon is not recorded. 'Daddy had a cardiac arrest,' might have improved the script somewhat, but lies unrecorded on the cutting room floor.

It seems that, unlike learning, wisdom can be gained in some rather more exciting ways. For example, I learnt to take care when climbing by falling off a cliff backwards. That was exciting let me tell you, as I only can tell you because my fall was broken by the large backpack I happened to be carrying. As I lay sprawled on my back among the angular beach rocks I turned my head to one side to find a sheep right next to me who had apparently tried the same trick without as much success. It was a visual reminder of how my bloated and decomposing corpse might have looked when discovered, in this remote spot, days later. It was a very direct form of education.

Similarly I learnt about the dangers of house fire from being even closer to death than I was to the rotting sheep. I was staying on a kibbutz in Israel (where else?), sharing a room with a school friend and coping with the heat, dust and stunning Israeli girls in the only way a boarding school boy could. No, not that, as far as I recall, but by drinking ice-cold beer and flirting with the Germans who happened to turn up. I'd never seen women with hairy legs before, so I was not attracted mind, but at least it passed the time.

Another time waster occurred in the smallest room. When you first entered, you were struck by the speckled-effect paint job. This is a remarkably nouveau riche touch to an otherwise Spartan environment. However, on closer inspection, for which there is a lot of time for stomachs used to food cooked by Mummy, a grim discovery is made. Every single one of the thousands of dots is a crushed, splattered or smeared mosquito. Another swarm has entered with you, and the next few minutes is spent is the enthralling game of mosquito hunting. All the wit and guile of the adult male is piled up against the little buzzing terrors until the last one joins the merry graveyard covering the whitewashed walls.

These nasty beasties not only followed us into the toilet but also stole a ride when we went into our oven, otherwise known as a bedroom. This box-sized room had no insulation and a meshed window facing south. Once the door was closed this kept the mosquitos out, but every night we would wake up with itchy lumps on every exposed surface, which in the stifling heat was pretty much everywhere. So I devised a simple plan. Each night I would burn a mosquito coil. This was a spiral of green cardboard, vaguely reminiscent of a flattened turd, which would smoulder for hours and provide long-term protection against the biting menaces.

One night I was particularly lazy and instead of changing my pillowcase just rested the new one on top of the unchanged pillow. Sometime in the middle watches I awoke. It seemed very dark so I reached for my watch to find out what ridiculously early time it was. Unexpectedly I could not see my watch as I held it in front of me. I reached over and turned on the light. I still could not see my watch so I lifted my hand to my face, only to realise that, even with my fingers practically touching my nose, my hand was invisible, shrouded in some thick murk. Only then did I realise the room was full of smoke and I immediately started coughing. It was a matter of moments to rush over to the bed of my friend and drag him out into the fresh air.

Being particularly stupid, I decided it was my duty to go back and prevent the fire spreading. So with dampened hanky over my nose, I returned spluttering into the smoke to retrieve the pillowcase from on top of the coil. Now here's the thing. As soon as it got to the outside air, it burst into dramatic flame, engulfing the whole in a moment of conflagration. You see, there was no oxygen left in the room. Had I not woken up at that exact moment, my parents, nay, both our sets of parents, would have received a letter informing them of the sad demise of their children, accompanied by a picture of our lifeless corpses, unsullied except for two utterly appalling beards. On second thoughts they may not have recognised us and spent the rest of their lives wondering how we were getting on in our new life in Israel.

What, you may well ask, has this got to do with learning? Well, it's a long way around to make a simple point. When I was young I was extremely reckless. Age has not changed my enjoyment of dangerous sporting pursuits. My character is as it was – not changed whatever. But a few dramatic incidents have made me someone who is very cautious. Finding yourself breathing when you really shouldn't be; or staring between your spread legs down at a sixty-foot drop onto rocks after slipping over on black ice and landing on the edge on your backside; or sliding half a mile in a perfectly straight line so that you miss the other car by inches; or being rescued just as your feet start to slip under a boat propeller (oh yes, I'm good at not quite dying). All these things change a man. They make him think. Not only the obvious, how am I so totally nuts? Not just, I should be dead? Nor even the most likely: Oh no, not again. They make him careful. They give him a healthy respect for danger. They don't change his character, but they certainly add something important.

At the other end of the spectrum, when being cautious involves holding the kettle with two hands to stop it shaking so much you splash hot water down your – probably already damp – trousers. Sorry, I got lost in a reverie all on my own there. I mean old age. At the other end of life, character also does not change – but it certainly appears to. Some old people do start to lose bits of themselves. And I don't mean limbs, though that does happen (and I'm really looking forward to that, I can tell you). They start to lose bits of their character. I vividly remember as an unsympathetic teenager, watching a distinguished guest arise to make a speech at a formal dinner, finish his brief talk, which was largely a version of thank you, and then start again at the beginning. His wife quietly and lovingly pulled him back down into his seat, and everyone carried on as if nothing had happened. But for almost all of us it was our first taste of dementia.

It did not affect our enjoyment of the meal. The turkey was already dry and dusty, as the cook was roped in practically off the streets to do for the boys (I vaguely recall that she did the school cleaning). But it made us think. One day that'll be me. And it could be worse. Some become violent, some incontinent, some just end up drooling. But I am not convinced they change character, it's just as if bits are being quietly subtracted. Sometimes it's the clever bits; sometimes the kind bits; sometimes the sane bits. And what's left over, just like the remnants at the end of our Christmas meal, is not pretty.

Some of us think of Down's Syndrome a bit like that. Somehow some of what is Caleb has been kept safe somewhere else. We've been left with all the best bits, which does make everything less of a trauma, but some of those other elements, which would stop other children from stepping off a cliff or walking fully clothed into a swimming pool, are just not here. Last week Caleb came wandering out of the living room without trousers. We went in expecting to find a wet patch on the floor by the telly where he'd been playing, but all was dry. Then I noticed someone had spilled a drink on the side table. "What did you knock over, darling…" And then my minimal brain cells kicked in. There was a lot of slightly yellow fluid and no cup in sight. Caleb had clearly felt the need to go, decided that he should go somewhere and then quietly taken down his trousers, stood on the table and let go. Not many children would do that. They have in built barriers. They have some sense that tables have a different function to toilets (I can't think why, it had a lip around the edge which neatly kept all the pee off the ground). Caleb doesn't. His common sense just isn't there. It, with a number of other faculties, is somewhere else and one day, I suppose, we may see the whole of him fully together as one complete person. But for now we must enjoy what we have, and enjoy it to the full. It's not as if we have someone that is less Caleb, as everything we love about Caleb is fully Caleb (so to speak). But we don't have all.

What we do have is surprisingly good at repetition. Test Caleb on the names of trains and he will be brilliant. Rather too often I am found in the dark, in my monkey suit (just don't ask), in the lounge doing 'names'. This involves picking up toy wooden trains from a yellow box and handing them to Caleb one after the other. He then names them and puts them carefully onto the track. This is relatively straightforward when it is a distinctive train like Gordon. Even I can do that! But some of them are virtually indistinguishable in the light. Dash and Bash only differ in colouring, which in the strange yellow light suffusing through our front curtains, is, let's face it, grey on grey. But Caleb can tell immediately. How? I've no idea.

And the other thing is that he never gets bored. I have a real problem with boredom. It infiltrates my life, here through marking endless tedious exam scripts, there through listening to endless tedious questions about what we are doing on Saturday. I'm even beginning to feel light-headed and more than a little sick as I pore over exercise books. But Caleb has an infinite boredom threshold when it comes to trains and cars. One of his favourite books is a list of the top 100 cars that make you go Phwaor! It's not very mentally challenging, but I do find myself idly reading the blurb as we go through, even getting a little bit interested in 'under-steer' and 'overdone carbs' or whatever. But no, that's not allowed. I just have to read the names, one after the other, over and over again. Now as we go down the road you'll hear Caleb quietly murmuring to himself 'beemwoo' or 'owdwi'. The passersby must think we're nuts. And we are - but, on the other hand, it's strangely satisfying. Maybe I should try it in place of marking. Just murmur 'brill', 'baws', 'duh' as I pass out the books. You never know they might at least think about the work rather than just clock the mark.

You would expect this ability to endure repetitive boredom would help Caleb with his learning. After all learning is repetition. But no, as every parent knows, children have an education radar. They know from the other side of the universe that education is about to be done to them and react accordingly. Balaam's ass could take lessons in being stubborn. Caleb has a particularly amusing way of dealing with the advent of education. He teases you mercilessly. He will pick random objects off every surface and fire them across the room. He will take whatever book you are reading and turn it upside down, or hold it just out of reach. He will even rip everything to shreds before your eyes as you impotently grab at it to try and prevent him, thus doing even more damage than he. The child who has spent two hours lining up the cars in rows on a table, will not spend thirty seconds lining up numbers just because he knows you want it and that this is learning.

If we could produce 'yootupe' videos featuring trains that taught him to read, I expect we'd have a success on our hands but as long as it is those inestimably weirdly named Chip and Biff books he's unlikely to get beyond Look. And while I'm on this little rant, why do they start with Look. In my day at least it was Peter and Jane. They did nothing more exciting than find the dog Pat up the tree, which used to send my poor mother into fits of giggles every time, but at least they began with words like 'and' and 'is'. Words, that is, which sound the way they are spelt. Unlike Look. Why not start them on 'through' or 'friend'? Or 'weird' and 'dumb' for that matter.

On the other hand Caleb is great at teaching. Put him in a room of fighting dogs and after a few seconds they'll all be surrounding him just to see what's wrong. He would in turn be exchanging licks with them. Oh yes, full on, tongue in the mouth, licks and soon there'd be a happy frolicking bundle. No one can change the atmosphere like Caleb. Yes, occasionally he gets it badly wrong - he thinks that a head butt in the teeth is a sign of affection - but a beaming smile, or a convulsive bout of tears and everyone wants to do what Caleb wants. I think it's something about the vulnerability. If you're with someone whose every emotion is broadcast to the world, and you know that there is no faking in it, then you just want to make him laugh or smile. Unless that is you happen to be his brother and have come off worst too often. A certain immunity is conferred by exposure on a regular basis, but even then they cannot hold out for long. The moment is over and they are soon drawn in to his happy world.

As I sit over my coffee and watch the pigeons outside scrabble at the cobbles for scraps of bread, I am drawn to wonder how much of our learning is much the same activity. Are we largely pecking at trifles in the hope that they will feed our fevered brains, or are we, as some hope, reaching out to the stars to grasp something of the vital nature of the universe? I had such a thought as I sat the other day studying theology. If it is as Robert Winston puts it, 'the recitation of the incomprehensible by the unspeakable to pick the pockets of the unthinking' then why am I bothering? Or is all knowledge like this? Is it just a type of brain exercise to keep our overactive minds from exploding?

And then it struck me. Ideas do matter. Not because they change who we are, or even change how we behave, but because they operate somehow at the interface of the two. Like little cellular proteins operating on genes, they switch on and off various aspects of our character, fundamentally altering all that we seem to others.

Now the great thing about Caleb is that this filtration system is pretty much non-existent. Because he has no barriers, none of his essential character is switched off by ideas. What you see is who he really is underneath. And what should make you all stop in your tracks is that that is not just OK, but really wonderful. Without ideas shutting off selves, things are pretty good. The Blackfoot Indians (I know, not from India, but I was brought up on John Wayne) had this idea that children with Down's Syndrome are some kind of window onto the divine spirit. I'm not sure about that, but I do know that they give an insight into what being in the image of God might really be like, because in them the image is clear - partial, yes - but clear. With us it's so hazy you're lucky to see beyond the interference, but with them, what you see is what really is.

Now, I would like to bring you one more step. If learning is repetitive, habit forming and dull. If wisdom arises from dramatic insights. If neither changes who we really are, but merely our expression of ourselves into this world. If ideas operate at the interface between me and my behaviour and simply allow through or keep back the preformed character that I was blessed with originally, then a few things are true.

First, my ultimate origin is not in a birth canal. It breaks through that feeble barrier into the womb and even beyond. Somehow in some way beyond imagining I am in that early ball of cells, me. Me just waiting to be allowed out, waiting for the opportunity to express who I am. Me in hope. Me in expectancy. Dormant but not different. Hidden but not incomplete. Just me. And if this is so then all that is done to me is only a building of barriers, not a changing of essentials. Those barriers may appear permanent, though many of us hope they are not. Those barriers may be deliberate or accidental, destructive or liberating, but they are not in some proper sense real.

Second, my ultimate value has nothing to do with my ability to operate in this world. I may have almost no route through the wall between me and the world and yet what shines through may be a ray of sunlight. I may be unaffected by limit or inadequacy, and yet what is seen may be so unclear as to be meaningless, so shadowed as to be nothing. My value to others now and for eternity is not how much but how clear, not how loud but how sweet, not how strong but how calm.

Third, my ultimate destiny is in some strange way assured. All that is destructive is set to be destroyed. All that is true is eternal and undiminished by the mess that is made of it by this world. I do not mean that I cannot choose to take into myself some of that which remains outside, or that I may not take absolute responsibility for all that I do. I mean that if I really seek the good, then I will not be disappointed. If I ask after the pure, I shall find it. And Caleb? Nothing will diminish his light, for nothing can get in. Somehow, there is something untainted about someone who takes and gives without barriers. This is not perfect morality (whatever that means). Maybe it is perfect reflection. How terrifyingly wonderful is that?

Living

As I sat tonight, scraping dog poo off my trousers, I wondered if the best way to give my poor long-suffering reader an insight into life with Caleb was to provide a twenty-four hour snapshot. A genuine one, that is, not some contrived and especially dramatic one. Beginning, I vaguely felt, with the dog poo.

The evening began badly. I had failed to say the right thing about the new dress. No, that is far too generous to me. I had said completely the wrong thing, and here's the real clincher, with the wrong face. It wasn't so much the questions about size and price – that could have been ok. It was the rather obvious implication that my dear long-suffering wife had bought it solely because it was cheap. I might as well have said, 'Why did you buy THAT?' I admit to a sinking feeling when I heard it had been half price, and was not completely blown away by the dress, but to reveal this in such a crass way was foolish in the extreme. I guess I just long for Alison to splash out on herself, to go full out to look beautiful rather than forever to be seeking bargains. She's worth it. She just doesn't know it.

Enter Caleb. Cuddles. 'Mummy happy now.' More cuddles. 'Mummy happy now.' Not really but it somehow did the trick and after the requisite forty minutes of pampering we were off to the party.

This had been a five o'clock do for families, but somehow it had migrated to seven o'clock, but was still for families, and Caleb was certainly going. The two eldest had been disposed of in various ways about the local town, leaving Caleb and his immediately older brother Ethan to walk with Mum and Dad to the centre of town. Somehow a simple game of 'bang' lasted and lasted. Ethan took the simple course of hiding behind me as we walked along, and Caleb ran rings around me going 'BANG' at very regular intervals. Ethan would simple reply 'missed' and the game went on interminably. As I had been expecting to have to carry Caleb all the way, this was glorious news for me. Ethan had to occasionally pretend to die in great agony to stop Caleb giving up altogether, but we must have progressed nearly half a mile before the words 'Daddy, carry, peas' were heard. By that time I was so delighted I'd got away with it for so long that I made no protest and picked him up for the short remaining distance of our journey.

The upstairs room was packed, boiling and very loud. Immediately we entered our dear friends found us a drink at the bar and we parked Caleb at a table with a game to play, while we chatted to our hosts. It is advisable with Caleb to always keep a weather eye towards him, just in case, and so we each kept scanning to see if he was fine. At one point we both turned away at the same moment and, on turning back, saw that his place had been vacated. Such an event is not unusual, you must understand, so there was no panic. He has a tendency to move off and we are used to it, especially in public. One second he is where you put him, the next he is not.

We immediately scanned the room, but to no avail. It was a small room and so the search was brief. No sign. Guessing he might have done a runner on account of the noise, I left the building by the steep stairs and went out into the courtyard. No sign of him. Thankfully the main bar had a glass wall, so I could easily see if he had made his mark there. No one was looking strangely at a small child making his way through the throng. The disruption would have been clear. So I left the building by the short passageway that connected the pub to the road. No sign. And then out of the corner of my eye, I saw movement. He had crossed the road and was making his way down the middle of the road opposite. 'Where are you going, my love?' I asked. 'Home. Too noisy.'

He had left the party and was taking himself the mile across town to an empty dark house, across two busy roads (or more probably, down the middle of two busy roads) all because it was too noisy. There you have life with Caleb in a nutshell. Unpredictable.

When I got him back, I took the obvious step of keeping him close – on my knee, in fact – and of giving him something to do – eating a chocolate cake. It was a party so I made no fuss when he just ate the icing off the top, though I was slightly unhappy to find some on my trousers. I was even more unhappy to discover, as I scraped it off, that it had a slightly sticky consistency not normally associated with chocolate icing. 'Is that dog poo, daddy?' asked Ethan, and sure enough, it was. Caleb had walked through a dog turd on his little adventure and proceeded to transfer it to my nice new red trousers.

So I handed him to his mother, having dutifully removed the shoe, and escaped to the gents. In it I found two men discussing the unaccountable shortcomings of their partners. It seemed to be the shortcomings of each other's partners, now I come to think of it, which in hindsight seems a little strange. It does not seem an obvious route to friendship to explain to someone how his wife is SO inconsiderate. Your own maybe – a sort of sharing of woes – but not each other's. In fact it seemed to be rather one sided now I recall. A precursor to a punch on the nose, I might suggest, not an amiable chat over a beer.

Anyway they left me to it, complaining that the loo smelt of pee. I could have told them it smelt of dog poo, but maybe their own verbal excretion was too smelly to notice. It took me ten minutes with paper and water and the industrial strength hand-drier to bring cleanliness to the shoe, my hands and my trousers, but afterwards I felt like some kind of conquering hero. I had braved the dog poo and won. I returned to acclaim. Not so, of course, but I felt better anyway.

Now Caleb is in bed. 'Milk, bimana, storwee' have all been done. We've had a brief game of 'sausage roll door' and 'trains, names' and I've left him to cries of 'stay'. Hopefully he's now asleep. The sound of our puerile rhymes echo in my head, as tiredness now starts to take hold of me too:

'Sausage roll john – goes on and on'

'Sausage roll curtain – closed for certain'

'Sausage roll bed – where I lay my head and snuggle with Ted'

'Sausage roll room – boom, boom, boom'

'Sausage roll bore – makes me snore'

And his brother's creation:

'Sausage roll lamp – very damp – potato tramp'

And the one it all began with:

'Sausage roll door – upon the floor – have some more'

I can still recall its first utterance. We were on a horse ride along the fields next to his riding stables. The sun shone, the bees buzzed. It was idyllic. And suddenly he came out with it. 'Sausage roll.' 'Sausage roll what?' someone asked. And Caleb made the obvious reply, 'Sausage roll door'. Being in rhyming mood, I added some lines and the game was borne. Played first thing in the morning and last thing at night it is the soundtrack to our strange life. It sounds nonsense and yet it is strangely satisfying. No one knows the meaning, no one can make sense of the words, but what matters is that we say them together, that we share in their sounds, that they live for us. And there we have it. A good way to end the first evening of this one day with Caleb, 'Sausage roll door...' Try it. You may also find it strangely satisfying.

Toynutt. It's almost the background rhythm of life in the Moody household. It used to be toytutt, which I rather preferred but went out of fashion a few years back. Now if he needs to go it's always toynutt. I found myself pondering the importance of toilet visitations about twelve hours later, when Caleb appeared clutching his bottom. You can tell that he needs to go urgently by the strength of grasp and, usefully, which kind by the position. Just grasping the front lightly and he needs a wee, but can probably hang on. Hand through the legs and some serious rucking up of the trousers and a poo is on the way: move fast or you may find yourself fumigating the lounge or even picking a lump off the floor, as happened the other day. It takes tidying up to a whole new level.

The morning has been fairly uneventful. Caleb had to be got from his room, which meant we had a little bit longer to lie in – nearly to eight o'clock, which is quite something in this household. On arriving in our bed for a cuddle, Caleb was subjected to a mild quizzing on his disappearance the night before. It emerged that he had a Plan.

This Plan was to Cross Dangerous Roads, go through shops, 'down, down, down', go through tunnel, 'up, up, up' and then to Watch (or Otch) Cars. It was all quite believable. Watching cars while sitting on a busy pavement beside an even busier highway is a favourite pastime, and sure enough on the way from home to the pub we had passed one of his most-loved spots. That it involved crossing two major roads bothered him not one bit. It bothered us a good bit more, but he would not be told. Of course he could cross busy roads: he had a Plan.

Breakfast is always the same on Sunday in the Moody household: Croissants, pain au chocolat and coffee for us, hot bread for Caleb. He likes to have the middle pulled out from between the crust of the par-baked baguettes, and eat it with a layer of jam or chocolate spread on top. Today it was strawberry jam, with the leftover licked unobtrusively off the plate afterwards. He turned to me at this point and said, 'Dun shown', which slightly rattled the old man. I thought I had got his lingo off pat, but this one was new to me. 'Dun shown' he repeated, and I got it. It was 'Godzone' – the children's group at church.

This much-loved weekly event, sees Caleb propelled into a room full of adults and children and young helpers, one of whom peels off to look after him. The lucky teenager gets a full body hug as a reward and I slightly suspect there may be a bit of a queue for the duty. An hour's playing toys with a loving and humorous child must beat trying to engage a gang of disenchanted 'my parents made me come' youth with slightly over-worthy Bible stories. The trouble is getting rid of Caleb at the end. He comes attached, wrapped around legs, going 'woof' in his best dog. All bribes fail but he permits being slowly prised off with little complaint.

On the way home, the talk turns to Christmas presents. 'All trains; blue trains; take-long trains; wooden trains.' This is a well-rehearsed list of desires. He has discovered a new make of toy train recently (curse those adverts) and wants, quite reasonably, to possess all of them. I think there are about fifty, and, because we save all his benefits, he could probably afford them in one go, but we feel spending a small fortune on one child might rather upset the others. So he'll get some trains, just not all of them. Anyway, he'll need the money later for more important things, like somewhere safe to live. I'm not sure a hundred toy trains will be much of a bargaining tool in the big bad world of adulthood. Actually, I can think of a lot of men who would appreciate such an offer. Maybe a whole box of trains is not such a bad idea.

After lunch I propose a go on the Wii. Caleb likes to play on something called Sports Resort, which contains a whole range of games from ten-pin bowling to Frisbee throwing. There is one slight oddity about the whole thing – he does not actually play any of them. It is all done vicariously through me. I am ordered to 'cut' or 'bash' or 'throw', while Caleb cheers or bounces up and down like some kind of yogic flyer who's had too much caffeine. He gets quite excited and loves the violent ones. I'm just appalled at how useless I am at all of them, throwing endless split pins, scoreless Frisbees and battling unconscious sword fighters.

I have to do enough to win mind you or he really complains, but it's pretty low grade. Then we get to something called Island Flyover. It's not a great game but it has a certain charm, with simple graphics and neat visages. I quite like looking for the sites that you are expected to collect. And Caleb? He just wants to crash. When the plane crashes there is a satisfying crunch and ping noise and the two pilots pop up into the air to return, like thistle down, on little parachutes. 'Cut engine, hit on grass, gain' is the cry, 'hit on water, gain, gain, gain'. After a few minutes of this I am suffering mental breakdown and suggest Caleb takes over. He's ecstatic and is gone for twenty minutes of idle crashing.

It is not that he is violent. Yes, he has been known to head-butt backwards. He will whack you around the face when made to stop watching television or computer. And he has been known to give a pretty mean scratch – I've seen some of the results. But he's not nasty. Show him the fruits of his labour, show him that you or someone else is upset and he'll immediately look distraught, immediately say sorry in his best English, and immediately expect to be friends again. He just likes bashing and smashing. Throwing stuff on the floor, whacking sticks at other sticks, pushing objects off the landing and over the bannister, are all grist to his mill. Oh and he loves to shoot people. Not for real, I might add, just for fun. So crashing planes is right up his street.

We went out to buy a Christmas tree today, just he and his mother and I. The other children were banned because my eldest son could not be there and he could not bear the thought of everyone else getting to choose a tree without him. The solution, we decided, was not to let anyone choose. This was a real blessing as last year the whole family had been given a say in the choice. What actually happened was this: everyone got a tree of his or her own except Dad. Not too expensive, as we've found a really cheap place, but the arguing, the stomping, the hard faces, the false (and real) tears, will all stick on my memory for eternity. No, this method was far better.

We did the usual thing when couples choose. Alison chose a tree within the first two minutes and we then spent about an hour deciding it was the right choice. Caleb meanwhile wanted nothing more than to hit things with a stick. These things had to be held by me, which was more than a little terrifying. His stick flailed past my eyes on more than one occasion. His aim is pretty poor, so the trick is to find something long that can be held far away from your face. When not hitting my fingers with a stick he was choosing the most enormous Christmas tree. 'That one,' he would say, and as we looked admiringly at a smallish scrubby little thing, 'no, not that one, that one.' Our eyes would rise and then rise again to a monster tree, more suited to a castle than our small semi.

We returned with a tree, which served as a car divider on the way back. This had a useful function as it prevented Caleb from accessing the gear lever. Changing gears at inappropriate moments has become a new pastime for him. One minute I'm pootling along in third when suddenly the car is free running, and I look down to see Caleb trying to force the gear lever into fourth. 'Go faster, Daddy.' Or more commonly, 'Take, Daddy.' He has this odd idea that every trip in the car is a race with every car in front (I can't think where he got that from?), so we have to pretend that we're winning. If someone in front turns off, we say, 'Wrong way' – because everyone else is, by definition, going the wrong way. And we have to keep explaining to him that we cannot simply crash past other cars in a queue of traffic. Mind you, maybe we should try. It would make an excellent excuse in court. Caleb told me to, Your Honour.

He demonstrated his propensity to mess-creating behaviour shortly after we arrived home with the tree. It seemed a good time to give everyone a break so he was allowed to watch the television in the front room. I'm not sure what was on but clearly not something exciting, because he whiled away the time by chewing a battery. He got quite far, really, making a very significant teeth-shaped dent, almost breaking through the metal cover to the acid underneath. Idly I wondered if maybe we could have sued for failure to put a warning on the packet, like that woman who made millions out of McDonalds. 'Do not bite. May contain acid.' Not that Caleb could have read it, but the money would come in handy.

It just shows that with Caleb you have to be vigilant all the time. There is no off switch, of course, but neither is there a guaranteed on switch. He may seem engaged and busy but it does not mean that three seconds later he's not off home across a busy road, looking for horses somewhere miles away across Blenheim Palace gardens, or chewing a battery to see what will happen. Thankfully we got a phone call to say that Alison's parents were on their way, and Caleb could be usefully employed watching out of the window.

It was a short visit, with Caleb's party trick with the train names Grandpa's highlight. Until, that is, he went to leave. Caleb went up to him, patted his tummy and said 'big'. Just to make the point he followed it up with 'fat'. Grandpa didn't mind. He's not fat, just a little rounded in the stomach, I might note, and Caleb was being brutally honest as only he can.

So ended twenty-four hours in Caleb's life. It was a quiet family moment like any other. Only a fish and chip supper and a bit of 'te-wy' left to go. Then it's 'miwuk' and 'bimana' in bed with stories, and sleep. I am sure there are many days just like it. It's just like normal life, only different. Differently normal. But good.

Education

It is funny how one person can change the world. I recently read Boris Johnson's biography of Churchill, in which he argues that without 'The Churchill Factor' there is a good chance that Britain would have capitulated to the Nazi war machine. It was compelling reading, or at least until Boris got a bit bored halfway through and rushed the last few chapters. Maybe his hair got in his eyes at the typewriter. You can almost imagine him bashing away on an old machine, quietly swearing to himself, "Oh God, only another 3000 words".

Still he did have a point. It is pretty clear that some individuals have a huge impact on the lives of others. Without Nelson Mandela, South Africa would likely have collapsed into an unending bloody civil war. Without Alexander, we would have had no countries ending in 'stan'. Without George W Bush we'd probably be living peacefully with some of the Middle East at least. Though I'm pretty convinced everyone leaves an indelible mark on the universe, some do more than others.

With Caleb's education, two individuals stand out from the crowd in this respect. Mr Goodfun realised pretty early on that Caleb was out to make the most of every moment, and knew exactly how to make the most of Caleb. A talented actor and artist, he made every day fun and every day full.

I recently had the privilege of watching Caleb and his peers act out A Midsummer Night's Dream. Only one word in three was audible, but the story was acted out clearly with every movement and gesture, not least Caleb's scene. It's the moment where the artisans, who have practiced their play in the wood on midsummer's eve to great Shakespearian hilarity, get to do it for the gentry. In it Caleb has to find his lover, who is suitably cross-dressed (more Shakespearian laughs), and dead, and then commit suicide with a plastic knife (gosh, Shakespeare must have had them rolling in the aisles with that one). Well, this brought the house down it was so wonderfully visual: a sweeping knife to the chest, a grand collapse on the floor, a last gurgle of his final breath. All due to the early acting lessons with Mr G.

He used to bring Caleb out to us in the playground. Often there would be a new word accompanied by big acting. One of my favourite of these was when Caleb announced that he had acquired a 'fancy'. This lucky young lady was the focus of Caleb's attention for at least a year. He had to sit next to her, he had to have a photo of her, she came to his parties; she even popped over to play a few times, though he commonly didn't know what to do when she arrived. I think she was quite lucky really, because a kinder, gentler, warmer companion than Caleb you could not hope for. But I'm sure the word was Mr G's. It was just typical of him to find a word that summed up Caleb's mood and character so well.

More impressive still to me was his wisdom as a teacher. He was only a lowly paid teaching assistant and yet he clearly understood Caleb's needs and education better than all the highly paid professionals and teachers around him. It was intriguing to see how much they bowed to his wisdom in meetings. Of course he could turn on an actor's voice of authority (gentle but firm), which helped, but it wasn't just that. He had a quiet understanding that they could not match, coupled with a simple belief that Caleb could do it. I am sure we owe much of Caleb's successful navigation of much of his early education to him.

Mrs Perfectlife was rather different. For some reason that we never could fathom she did not seem to like our children. One child after the other had found themselves on the wrong end of her power to leave out, overlook or undermine. Now I'm a teacher and I know that parents can feel unfairly victimised without any genuine reason, but we never have felt this before or since from anyone else, and we had good reasons. In her defence, I'm not sure it was personal. We asked our daughter about it once. Her reply? 'It's not that she doesn't understand Caleb. She just doesn't understand children'. She had favourites who could do no wrong and victims who could do no right. Our children just all happened to be victims. She was pretty, talented and apparently happy. It didn't seem fair and we were desperate that Caleb should not fall under her spell.

Thankfully he ended up in the other class. Let me explain. Each year group had two parallel classes, that worked together, but had separate teachers. We were relieved. Until the first incident.

Caleb had, apparently, attacked a boy and tried to take his crisps, and Mrs P had decided to take him off on his own and sit him down so that he missed his break. I was incensed. Not only was it not credible that Caleb had attacked a boy like that, but there was little likelihood that taking away his break would make any sense to him, or change his behaviour, and anyway what on earth had it got to do with Mrs P?

So we did what no one else seemed to have done and asked Caleb. It turns out he thought the boy had stolen the crisps from another child and he was trying to get them back. From his point of view he had missed his break, which was precious to him, because he had tried to help another child.

When we went in to complain we discovered a pattern. The teachers were allowing the boys to play a bit more roughly to 'get them used to senior school', but Caleb was taking it too far and getting into trouble. From his point of view, he was just joining in the fun, but because he didn't have the usual boundaries he ceaselessly got into trouble. And the teachers seemed incapable of trying to understand him. In their view they were getting him ready for senior school and he needed fixing now before he moved up. Even the other children started to pick up the vibes, starting the rough and tumble and then complaining when Caleb rough and tumbled back

When we pointed out that he was going to special school so he didn't need to be got ready, they didn't listen. When we noted that allowing rougher play was simply setting Caleb up to be told off (how on earth did they think he would pick up normal boundaries? Had they not noticed he was DISABLED!), they didn't listen. When we advised them that removing his play was not an effective response to the problem, they didn't listen.

Don't get me wrong. This wasn't merely prejudice against a disabled child, there was good old-fashioned sexism as well. Mrs P was always pleasant to me, but she and Caleb's form teacher accosted Alison one day as she went in to pick up Caleb and did the double act on how we were wrong and they were right. Effectively how, if only we were good parents like they were going to show us how to be, then Caleb would be biddable and look like a good child.

So I went to the Head, and then they did what they were told, but we could tell Mrs P knew better. She just needed to impose on Caleb her perfect form of discipline and he'd change. After seven wonderful years at this school we spent the last year trying to ensure he wasn't badly affected. Thank goodness children are so resilient.

We had tried mainstream schools. The first interview was less than amusing. 'Was Caleb compliant?" seemed to be his main requirement. Well of course he wasn't compliant, because he had character. You're a teacher not a production manager, I wanted to scream at him. But we soon found out he wasn't even that.

His aim seemed to be to get children into the school who would easily provide 'added value'. This may confuse anyone not in the teaching profession, who might wonder how you can add value to a human being. The answer is you can't, but somehow the government decided it was a useful phrase to assess how well a school served its pupils. Did they come out having got better than the general trend of improvement with age? Someone with no understanding of Mathematics must have come up with that one, because clearly not every child can do better than average otherwise it's not average any more. But as English education is generally run by people who understand nothing about education this was no surprise.

What is far more disturbing than the ambition is the phrase 'value-added' used to express it. Someone clearly believed, albeit subconsciously, that doing well at school does make you more valuable. I get that you might be more successful or useful, though I think even that is quite doubtful (my most successful brother-in-law is a plumber), but it certainly does not make you more valuable. By that measure Caleb is completely valueless, and it was pretty clear that is exactly how our interviewer saw him. He was not even going to make education first base, let alone be fodder for some programme to get him up to speed.

So we left. We could have made a complaint as he was required by law to include Caleb and he made it very plain Caleb wasn't welcome. We could have got him sacked, as he showed us personal files on some of his pupils so as to show off his brilliant administration. We could have made a fuss. But we didn't. We just went on and tried the next school, where the Special Needs department was run by one of Caleb's previous professional helpers.

Well, you can imagine our surprise when she made it clear that Caleb would not be welcome there either. I don't mean she didn't want us, just that she told us plainly the school didn't want us, as Caleb would not improve enough to bring credit to the school. Indeed, she revealed that the money allocated to Caleb would be redirected by the school to children who would improve enough to bring credit to the school. She pretty much advised us that we would be better to home school him as at least then the money would be ours to use as we wished.

The third school gave us the warmest of welcomes. "We will do everything we can to help Caleb, should you decide to send him here." It was one of those effusive welcomes where you get no chance to ask any questions or indeed say anything at all for quite a few minutes, but it was certainly more positive. Then we went on a tour. We found out that Caleb would probably end up sitting at the back of a class on his own with no support. We found out that after two years they would have absolutely nothing available to support him. We found out that the site had no effective gates, so if he didn't like school he could just wander off home, crossing busy roads on his way. We found out that for all the warmth of welcome and passionate desire to help, the money allocated for his care would fund practically nothing.

We left despondent. All our expectations of mainstream education were dashed. Whatever the professionals of the town council and the amateurs of the Down's Syndrome Association said, mainstream education was a non-starter. We could sacrifice our son to prove a point or we could find a special school for him.

So that's what we did. Paperwork. Interviews. Paperwork. Meetings. Paperwork. Visits. And then the letter. He had a place at the best special school in the country, the ideal place for him. Thank you, oh thank you God.

Picture this six months later. The environment is warm and welcoming. Three teachers sit on those tiny chairs you find in classrooms. We are shown a video of Caleb greeting his peers in the very same classroom. 'He was reluctant to work at first, but now he's joining in.' 'He is wonderful in the play. He speaks his lines with such enthusiasm.' 'Here's his work. We love having him.' It was such a contrast it brought tears to my eyes. I even got asked how I dealt with him when he was reluctant to move on from one activity to another and my answer was valued.

If only I could have shown it to Mrs P. This is how you deal with Caleb. Mind you she'd have still thought she knew better. Maybe better to show Mr G. He'd have loved it all. Really he should work there. Better still he should give talks on how to do it. These teachers had extra training, extra money, extra facilities. He just had love and talent and passion. He's the one I'd give the biggest prize to. In a way he's got it, because none of us will forget him. Least of all Caleb.

I have just returned from a trip to the library with Caleb. On my own this takes about twenty-five minutes including choosing a DVD and walking there and back. Caleb has a curious irregular walking habit, where he dawdles for a while and then rushes for a few steps. This slows things down somewhat. Even then you'd expect to be through in twice the time, however long it takes to choose a DVD. This trip took us an hour and a half.

The first sign it would be slow was when he decided we should go through the wood. It's a little belt of overgrown woodland with a very narrow stream just by our house. It's a lovely place to walk, attractive to dog walkers and untamed youth alike. But it is emphatically not on the route to the library. So we wandered through it.

At the next place of choice, I pointed the way to the library. So Caleb took me the other way. I am still a little confused as to why. I think it may be because he was now on a familiar route, the one that usually takes us to Waitrose, the local supermarket. He may have simply preferred to follow the trammels in his mind and let his feet lead us. As we got closer to Waitrose, it seemed an ideal opportunity to stop for a bun and a coffee. So after some persuasion we did that, he for a sparklingly yellow iced bun, me for a virtually free coffee.

At last he seemed ready to head towards the library. It was a matter of only twenty minutes to find it, select a favourite DVD to take home and leave, out into the bright winter sunshine.

The walk home takes us past a letterbox. Unusually it is set into a wall, with a slot at Caleb's head height inviting him to post something in. So he did. The DVD, which we had spent an hour collecting, was slid purposefully into the hole in the wall. I'm not sure what he expected. I suspect he thought I'd be able to just open the box and get it back out. I am sure he had no idea we'd have to wait around for four hours and then try to persuade the nice postman to break all the rules and give it back. Thankfully for this scenario, I saw it going and grabbed it just in time. But it was a near thing. And he was pretty determined.

I tell this story to make a simple point. For Caleb and us his education is never going to be about getting exam results or achieving value added. It will always be about learning to live fully in that strange conglomeration we call society. It will help if at some point he realises that posting DVDs into letterboxes is not a good idea, or that buying ice lollies when you're not going home for another hour might not work.

I also slightly suspect that this is something he might be able to teach us. I am in education and I love the cut and thrust of the classroom. I adore the fascination of studying complex and challenging ideas. I revel in the practicalities of getting the best out of disinterested students. But I am pretty sure that real education is about enabling my students to live fully in the world. Learning will help, the disciplines of study and exams will help, but first and foremost will come relationships, and frankly Caleb is better at that than any of them. Now there's value added!

If you want your students to be really successful then you need people like Caleb in your schools. The students need to know what it is like to live and learn with people with additional needs. They need to see what it means to care for more than study (and to be honest, so do many teachers). They need to be surrounded by people who put relationships first, so they learn that relationships are first. They need Caleb. What a shame they don't want him.

Puberty

I had the strange experience of discussing bodily hair with one of my teenage sons in the car yesterday. This is the same son I had the sex talk with so maybe there was some precedent. The sex talk was simple.

'Dad, how do you get babies?'

'Well, the man puts his willy in the woman's front bottom and wiggles it about a bit.'

'Urgh, that's disgusting!'

'Yes, I suppose it is.'

He was about six, so I suppose it did the trick.

The hair chat was a little more complicated, not least because he is eight years older, but also because it was more directly relevant to him. We were particularly taken with his willingness to discuss the relative maturity of some of his friends. Frankly we kind of said, 'Urgh, that's disgusting' because we had some vague idea that they'd been comparing bits in the shower. It quickly transpired that this was not the case, but it was more about inferring from obvious secondary sexual characteristics. The signs were hair on the face or under the arms, not hair on the penis; a dropped voice, not dropped balls.

Nevertheless it became pretty free and easy, and not just a little personal. 'Dad, you've got no hair at all, so I'm a bit stuffed, aren't I?' I felt I needed to protest a bit. 'I've got hair on my chest' 'Yeah, about three' I had to admit that this was pretty accurate. Indeed since I first hit puberty, I'd been keeping a bit of a tally. I seemed to be getting a few more in later life, almost into double figures. I suppose they were migrating from my head, or something.

After this the conversation thankfully moved onto the age at which puberty hits. I was ok on this one, as I'd been pretty much

113

in the middle of my peers. That perfect position where you don't find yourself growling among the choirboys, or squeaking in the public bar. My son was a little worried he was going to be the last squeaker in the school. I of course assured him it was quite normal to take your time over puberty, telling him the story of a friend who had to wait until he was seventeen. I mentioned that he'd rather made up for it later, but this didn't seem to help, and indeed got a sharp look from Alison (or maybe I imagined that).

You see the problem is not that one son is late, which he isn't, but that another is early. Caleb has hit puberty like a train hitting the buffers at high speed. He has the deep voice, the hairy willy, the lot, and he's over two years younger.

Initially this came as a pleasant surprise. My children seem to have generally done teenage angst the wrong way round. As pre-teens they have been loud, grumpy, uncommunicative and rude. When teenage hormones hit they did not exactly become angels, as they now had all those worries about exams and careers that we delight to load them with, but they did oddly cease to act like teenagers.

Caleb was no exception. In the years leading up to puberty he had become increasingly difficult to manage. I have a permanently damaged front tooth from a head butt to the mouth to show for it, but that was minor. If we wanted him to move from playing with trains to eating supper, then he would kick and scream. He'd attack with feet, usually covered in those huge Piedro boots, so a really deadly weapon. He'd hit, head butt, bite, throw things across the room. Sorry but it's true. With Caleb, because there are no filters or barriers, you get the real child coming out full throttle. I was sent in because I'm still relatively strong. He might have genuinely hurt Alison.

This is where I could get into trouble. I did once try a smack. Not hard, not angry, not anywhere vulnerable you understand, but I thought it might work. Well, he just hit back. And that's the first lesson I learnt. He just thought I was hitting him, so his natural defence was to hit back. He had no filters to stop him. He reacted completely naturally, the way every child would if they didn't have all those social conventions hanging over them. If we smack a child, we are hitting them: why shouldn't they hit back? And if they don't what are they doing with the desire to hit back. It doesn't make a child meek and obedient, it makes them secretly angry. At least that's my view.

The equivalent in the classroom are teachers that shout. Now, there's nothing wrong with a raised voice to get attention, make it clear of your disapproval, show who is boss. But shouting is different. It's when aggression is focused on an individual. It can bring quiet, but it breeds anger and aggression. I found it always better to find a better way. If you build students up, make the lessons interesting, and set very clear expectations then they are much less likely to cause difficulties.

With Caleb I found the best, indeed the only, technique was to give love and time. If he really got cross I would hug him until he stopped. If he was reluctant to move then I would jolly him with humour and distraction. If nothing else worked I would persistently require him to do as asked and he almost always eventually came round to my way of thinking. I might have to remove the distraction and then remove everything else so he had nothing to break, but once I'd got him focused on how much he was loved, and gave him the time to change his way of thinking, he would move. I have some scars to show for it, but then real love often leaves scars I find.

So puberty was a delight. He is still reluctant to move and we have some broken crockery to testify to his outbursts, but he is so much easier. But there was another surprising benefit.

I don't know what your worries would be for a disabled child, but mine varied from the sensible to the absurd. On the sensible side, I am concerned about his transition into adulthood. Will he be able to leave home? Will he ever get work? Will he find a wife, who loves him? These have largely been assuaged by the realisation that I have exactly the same concerns for all my other children. In today's world none of these things are the least bit certain.

On the silly side, I was worried about his willy. When he was little you could hardly find it. He had three little currant-sized lumps, out of one of which squirted yellow stuff. It really was miniscule. I'd had two boys before so I knew what I was expecting and it just wasn't there. 'Will he even be able to pee standing up?' I wondered. If there was not enough to get hold of then he'd have to sit down like a girl for the rest of his life. Not exactly the end of the world, but remember that boys really do have pissing contests. I can't imagine Caleb ever being asked to join in, but it wasn't in my mind a minor problem.

Then came puberty. Now I want to be clear on one thing. I was not watching his penis to see if it was growing. He was of an age where he still needed help with using the toilet so I guess I must have been aware of his bits, but I just didn't register any changes. As a result it came as rather a shock when Alison said something like, 'Have you noticed Caleb's willy? It's enormous.' And it was. Really quite huge. Disproportionately large.

With two other teenage boys, I have the occasional surreal conversation about average sizes. They seem to be a bit concerned about height, which I suppose is not surprising. One is very tall, so quite happy to talk about height. The other is normal height and weight but windsurfs for the country so is fairly obsessed with body size and how it affects his performance. So we end up wondering about where they are compared to the average for their age. Average penis size also

116

comes into it. At the school sex talk, they get given some statistics which are meant to calm their nerves, though, like most of the stuff in sex talks, probably has the opposite effect to that intended. I imagine there were lots of boys with rulers later that evening, just checking under the covers. Something they never even thought about like penis size, or how to put on a condom suddenly acquires unnecessary significance.

As a dangerous aside, what is the point of showing boys how to put on a condom? The sex talk tutors seem to see it as one of their roles, but I'm never sure of the point. For one, it tells you in every packet. There're even little pictures. Not coloured thankfully, but they do make it pretty clear. For two, it's pretty obvious. You just roll it down the stick. For three it's pretty useless. They seem to imagine you suddenly sitting up in the middle of coitus and carefully ripping open the little packet and slowly putting on the condom. What, I wonder is your partner doing at this stage? Maybe she can have a quick read of her trashy novel, while you take your time. I don't know, but what I do know is this: you're going to need to start the whole thing again from scratch or even, if you're like me and unlucky, give it up and have another go tomorrow.

What the sex tutors really need to do is this. Turn the lights off and close the curtains so it's really dark. Tie one of your hands behind your back and cover you up with some suffocating blankets. Now make it a race. Who can rip open the packet with their teeth fast enough so the flow isn't interrupted but slow enough not to rip the contents. All the while you have to make excited noises through your clenched lips and inscribe small circles on the floor with your free hand. You have two minutes. Go. Now that would be worth practicing until perfect!

Caleb has discovered his large penis and this has led to a whole new set of concerns. He realised quite a long time ago that it was soft and warm and squidgy which made it an ideal place to put your hands at night. Now he's found out that if you wiggle it about enough it sticks up. While this is no surprise to his Dad, you understand, I am not at all sure how to deal with it. Especially as at some point in the near future he is going to discover that if you wiggle it about enough it does something even more surprising.

My main line so far has been to encourage him to value his penis, but to see it as a private affair. 'Yes, it's very beautiful but not in front of...urgh, do leave it alone' or words to that effect. I have an odd memory of my Dad objecting rather sharply to me holding on for warmth as quite a young child. It's one of my earliest memories (which says something worrying about me I suspect) and I don't want Caleb's early memories to be similar. So I'm very careful not to be sharp, but his thing is really big, and it can be a bit of a shock to see it on such full display.

I would turn to the books on sex and Down's Syndrome, of which there are a few, but I am rather distrustful of books on sex. It is pretty clear to me that sex education in the UK at least has had no beneficial effects whatsoever. The model often sited to show it works is the Scandinavian one. Here they have lots of sex education and few teenage pregnancies. It is thought that we can learn from it. I am not so sure. Not least I am deeply suspicious of the idea that correlation equals cause. They may have lots of sex education and they may have few teenage pregnancies but that does not mean one causes the other. There are lovely examples of these. My favourite is the apparent correlation in the UK between the amount of cheese bought and the revenues enjoyed by golf clubs.

Even if it works for the Scandinavians though, there is no reason to suppose it works for us, and the evidence is definitely lacking that it has done so. Indeed I suspect you could correlate increases in sexually transmitted infections and sex education. I am not suggesting one causes the other, though it might be the case, but merely that one cannot assume two facts connected only by their relationship to sex are causally connected.

My own sex education at school was very revealing. It taught me that my biology teacher found the whole thing incredibly embarrassing for he went beetroot red whenever it came up in the course. It also taught me that videos of partners coupling (in cross-section of course - this was the 1980s) were pretty strange. We'd have been better off watching Monty Python's The Meaning of Life.

I suppose my view on sex is pretty simple. If you get used to it, then you need it regularly. If you don't get any then you can get by pretty well without it. Oh and without real, proper, permanently committed love, it'll all end in tears. And I don't mean by that to be flippant. Sex has a very special place and it's best for everyone if it's kept there.

But how does that help with Caleb. Well I suppose I'd like him to find a wife. Any woman would be lucky to have him, as she would never lack for love. In the meantime though he's best left to it. If fiddling with his willy is amusing and comforting who am I to stop him? Just please keep it covered. The sight of something that big would frighten the living daylights out of some people.

Travel

I am on a journey. Not a metaphorical one but a real one. As I write this I am on a coach on my way to Heathrow to fly to America.

I love journeys. I love the anticipation of new things. I love the brief random conversations with strangers. I love the sights and sounds of new places. I even love the smells. As a student I went with a friend to Israel. I still remember, over thirty years on, the moment that the doors opened on our aircraft as it stood on the tarmac at Tel Aviv's Ben Gurion airport. The buzzing cicadas, the steamy heat and the rich organic Mediterranean smells. There's nothing quite like it.

On this journey I travel alone. It's midweek and the family are busy. I'm visiting old friends so they'd be bored even if they could come. And I could get a good car for the price I'd have to pay for the six of them. So it feels very like those early student journeys.

It would be much better with Alison. Someone to share the whole adventure doubles the fun and halves the hassle. But I can't. And here's the difference children make. Until they are of an age where you can go off and leave them you don't get to travel as a couple. With generous relatives this age can be quite young. But not with Caleb, or at least so we've found. The relatives are less willing to look after him, the age at which he can be left is older and, more to the point, he doesn't like being without us.

So our first holiday together as a married couple since our daughter was born nearly ten years ago was last month. As it happens my parents found it a lot easier than they expected, so we may go again. Caleb has at last reached an age where he can be left. Sadly this almost exactly matches the age at which my parents are too old to look after him. Hey ho.

So here's my point. When it comes to holidays Caleb changes things. But so do my other children. In particular one son who competes for Great Britain as a windsurfer. His windsurfing has taken us all around the country. It has taken us to Italy, Sardinia and Poland. It has taken over our holidays. But have we missed out? No, not one bit. We have made new friends, seen new places. We are called performance patients, though my performance is often to act like I know what's going on, and it sucks up huge quantities of time and money - but we've gained, not lost.

With Caleb it can feel a little different. Over the last year we got into the habit of not taking him because it 'wouldn't work'. I think we meant a number of things by this. First, he just wants to be at home. In Italy two years ago we counted down from thirteen 'sleeps'. Second, it inevitably reduces our options. He walks, but not far. He swims, but not for long. He doesn't really like the beach. All he really wants is to eat ice cream and play with his trains. Third, he doubles the luggage. On the Italy trip we booked in a whole extra hold bag just to fit in his trains and books.

So we tended to separate. One of us stayed home with Caleb, while the other went away. And it felt like that: separation. If we went we enjoyed the trip, but not as much. If we stayed, we enjoyed being with Caleb, but missed the trip. So after the last one, I was clear. Never again would we let Caleb separate us in this way. We could split up and do things apart, but not because of Caleb.

I'd learnt a simple lesson. Life is about love, not experience. Experiences are great and a wonderful backdrop to friendship and love, but life is lived to the full in relationship. And so I'm off to America. Not to see the Grand Canyon, though if I ever get the chance I will rush at it. Not to see the USA. I know many people love it but I can take it or leave it myself. No, I'm off to see my beloved younger brother and one of my best friends. If fun happens all to the good, but I just want to be there with them.

A close friend put it like this. He had a picture of a clear space, like a table covered with a simple cloth but empty of everything else. And on it, dead centre is a figure. It is as if Caleb has cleared the table, in his usual fashion of just punching everything off it and onto the floor, and there in the middle is left the only thing that matters. A person. A friend, a brother, a wife, a husband, a son, a daughter. On display for me to see, so I know what really matters.

Without Caleb, I'm not sure I'd have ever seen this. His presence could seem to be a kind of loss because there is much we cannot do. But in reality he has exposed what really matters. We can get so caught up with the adventure, we forget who we are travelling with. I for one am travelling with Caleb. Not today, that's true. But through this life, not least because he has taught me true value. And he can teach you too.

As I sit at my window seat, I wonder if I'm rather overdoing it. I am off on my own for a few days and if Caleb were here I would not be able to close my eyes and nap, or stare for long minutes at the country laid out below me, or write this. While this is true with any child, it is more true with Caleb. If you don't watch him anything may happen.

A short while ago I was left in charge of the house. Caleb had wanted to go to the train shop in Oxford but we had to delay the trip. We have only one car and it was being used. So Caleb took himself off upstairs to his room to read his Thomas books, while I took a five minute break.

Thus a little while later I could be found sitting in our front room overlooking the little square of grass that we share with five other houses. I think I may even have been watching daytime TV, that destroyer of all mental faculties. Lo and behold, our neighbour appeared at the window, looking more than a little perturbed and towing Caleb behind her.

On opening the door, the mystery deepened. He had been found by a stranger wandering down the road about a hundred yards away. The stranger noticed something odd about this little boy. Not only was he young and alone and looking a little different but he was in his pyjamas. So he accosted a passing woman for help which just happened, oh thank you God, to be our neighbour.

After getting him inside I did a little investigation. His pyjamas had an angled dirt mark on one side. On lifting the edge, I found a nasty scrape. So I asked him about it. 'Oxford' he said, 'trainshop'. Ah so he has assuaged his disappointment at not being taken by trying to go himself. I had to applaud his independence.

But one thing bothered me. How had he got out. The room I was in overlooked the front door, and I'm afraid that the eternal and indistinguishable property programmes could not have gripped enough to stop me noticing a small pyjama'd child exiting through our rather noisy door. 'Window' he said.

Well now I was really confused. We had recently had a spate of finding his bedroom window wide open, and, out of fear for his safety, had locked the first floor windows and put the key in a safe place. So I looked. Sure enough his window was wide open. But there was no way he could have got out that way. It was twenty feet vertically to some crazy paving, with nothing to hold onto, and then there was a high locked side gate in the way.

I looked further. The landing window was also ajar. The bushes by the drainpipe were flattened. Now it was clear. He had found the key and opened his own window. On realising it was too far down, he had opened the landing window, climbed down onto the porch roof, scrambled down the drainpipe next to it, and landed on the shrubbery below. All to get to the train shop. Bless him.

I am on another journey. This time by train, travelling the Amtrak from Chicago to St. Louis. As I sit here, I ponder whether I need to say something about beauty. Please don't get me wrong. Caleb is attractive in a perfectly everyday way. He has very neat symmetrical features, a winning smile and, according to my son, perfect eyebrows. But even Caleb's appearance will frighten some people. He looks different.

I once used this to our advantage.

'Have you got some proof of disability?', the woman at the till asked. We'd just had the effrontery to ask for exit passes at Legoland, and she was a bit suspicious.

'Just look', I said, and held him up to the window. I may have imagined it but I thought I heard an audible 'pop' she moved so fast after that. We had so many exit passes we hardly knew what to do with them.

For me it was a badge of honour to have a child that looked special, but I am not too naive to realise for others it is a terror. The spirit of the age values looks above almost anything else, and to be unattractive to others incurs a huge disadvantage in every walk of life. Disability almost always confers this double burden of lacking looks and ability.

The worst aspect of this in my view is how it encourages the young to despise themselves. They inevitably see themselves as unattractive, with rare exceptions, and so avoid being photographed, or spend forever making themselves up, or even end up in a spiral of self-destruction.

Ever since Norman Vincent Peale's book *The Power of Positive Thinking*, authors and publishers alike have been making vast profits from self-help books that purport to help with life. In this case, though, it seems to me that they are worse than useless. In such circles, the mantra seems to be to learn to love the way you look. To look in the mirror and love the visage that looks back.

Unfortunately it seems to me that this is fundamentally flawed. Neither God nor nature designed us to find ourselves attractive. We are aligned to the opposite. For man 'no suitable helper could be found' so God made woman, both alike yet different. If we look at ourselves and are attracted then that is in some ways unnatural. I think this is one reason even our icons of beauty often have poor body image. Of course you think you're ugly, I want to call at them, there'd be something wrong with you if you didn't.

What Caleb offers is a way out of this. He knows he's beautiful for one simple reason. The mirror he sees himself reflected in is my face. The looking glass that looks back at him says you're beautiful because I love you, and he can read it in every wrinkled feature of my face. Our attraction is written in the eyes of those whom we love and who love us. While we look for ourselves in photographs, Caleb looks for mummy and daddy. Well, that is unless there's a train.

Caleb is not easy. He's a challenge. But he's worth it, and for me here's the reason. Last night I was out at a meeting. Caleb thought I had left for America already, so when I got home I got a hug. But not a normal one. This one involved every part of his body. Arms and legs wrapped round me. Cheeks pressing to mine. The broadest of smiles accompanied the one word, 'Dad'. Love is worth any amount of hassle. And Caleb is so full of it, it floods out everywhere. Now that is a thought worth holding on to.

The Future

As a child I was fascinated by space travel. It seemed to me then that the future of our planetary population lay among the stars. Who from that era of flares and long hair cannot, with me, remember how even the incredibly rickety sets of TV's Space 1999 seemed like science fact. One day we would be living on the moon, wearing shell suits made from shiny silver nylon and flying upside-down egg boxes across the lunar surface. It seems absurd today when you look back (and how it did not seem absurd then, I'll never know), but it all appeared to be mankind's natural destiny. I certainly wanted to be part of it. If I hadn't got bad eyesight and had the misfortune to be born British, I'd have been off to NASA like a shot from a gun.

Now we know better. The future will see us all forced back to the stone age as the oil runs out, the seas flood all available arable land and nuclear weapons fall into the hands of religious terrorists. Soon it will be every man for himself. I guess we have to thank God we are saved from those appalling haircuts that seemed to be de rigueur for all science fiction programmes, and the totalitarians are unlikely to maintain control so it's a lot better than 1999 or 1984, but hardly what we hoped for our children. We wanted robots to do all the menial jobs (and a little light murder on the side to keep things interesting, if Isaac Asimov is to be believed), bodies like iron without the lifting of same, and interplanetary travel as a form of light entertainment. Instead we've given our future offspring the likelihood of endless backbreaking labour interspersed with international conflict. Great.

I will say one thing for all these visions of the future, whichever may in the end be prescribed for us. None of them seem to have any place for disability. With the odd exception of Professor Charles Xavier in the X-Men, who makes up for it with mental brilliance (how stereotypical is that?), the weaknesses of all these fictional characters seem to be a bit like those of Dick

Francis's heroes, invented, imaginary, unreal. Well, let me tell you, in real life disability is everywhere. My teeth seem to be falling out, my knees work not a lot, my insides are a law unto themselves and my hearing and eyesight are slowly fading. And I'm pretty healthy. Real life does not include some magically 'scientific' fix for all our difficulties but a troubled living with them. We all have them as soon as we reach an age where we know our arse from our elbow (at about 35, I think) so why do we have so much trouble accepting them in others? Why do we fictionalise them out of our visions of the future?

Do you ever cry? I cry quite often. I cry as I watch a movie. It doesn't have to be clever or deep, just soppy or sweet. I cry when the simple miseries of everyday life pile up behind the eyes and have to be let out one way or another. I cry when something goes wrong for my children, a lost chance, a deep unfairness, a simple hurt. But just now I cannot stop myself crying. It began as I watched a film of adults with mental disabilities being abused and tortured by their care workers. It grew as I watched their parents sit open-mouthed in shock as they viewed the documentary footage. I cried for them but I also cried for my Caleb. In a world obsessed with strength and beauty, what place will there be for someone whose greatest talent is to be vulnerable and gentle?

The Winterbourne View care workers have been punished. The government has promised to bring in new legislation. The newspapers have had their self-righteous outcry (oh no, we never bully anyone). 'We must make sure that this never happens again (again)'. This is all very nice but you have to wonder how it happened in the first place. These care workers were not particularly evil people. Most were genuinely horrified by what they had done. There was no lack of money to pay for good care. Each resident was being supported by a sum approximately equal to almost eight times the national average earnings. One could blame the ringleader, an appropriately mythical figure, tattooed, shaven-headed and malicious, who prowled and ruled. Even that seems a little harsh. Bullies need to be free to bully, and a hospital is not the obvious place to experience such freedom.

You might think I want to blame the owners from the above, but not really. True they were clearly greedy and mendacious, taking vast profits for themselves while deceiving staff into believing that they had to work long hours for low pay. And they've got away scot free, which somehow seems more awful than all the rest. But it is very unlikely that they intended vulnerable adults to be effectively tortured. I don't mean by this that they are good people. Crush their balls in a nutcracker would be my advice. I just don't mean that they can take the blame in its entirety, and nor can any one of the guilty parties. It all runs a little deeper than that.

There are the adults with learning difficulties trained by the terrorists as suicide bombers. Sent strapped into an explosive vest into a crowded place, with little idea of what's going on and then detonated remotely by their handlers. There is the case of an older teenager smashed in the face by some of his peers just because they could, just because he was bigger than them but had no clue about defending himself, let alone fighting back. There are the orphans, whose East European parents have abandoned them to be brought up in homes, who have no rights, no opportunities, no protectors, who are treated worse than animals, left to die in their own faeces just because they lack certain abilities.

This is one vision of the future for my Caleb. As I watched him pretend to be a dog and play fetch with a young helper at his Scout group, I wondered: How will that work when Caleb is fully grown? Will the same young lad be quite so sanguine when a full-sized adult grabs him round the leg and refuses to let go? Will he then find it amusing or annoying throwing a paper plate for Caleb to pick up in his teeth to bring back to his hand? Without Dad there to carefully detach the young puppy and take him back to a loving home, how will the young man really respond? I wonder. I hope but I also fear.

In July 1961, a young social psychologist began a series of tests to examine how far normal people will submit to an authority figure. In the experiment a teacher is required by an experimenter to test whether punishment helps a learner to remember a series of simple word lists. While on the face of it both learner and teacher are volunteers, the selection is in fact fixed so that the true subject always ends up the teacher, while the learner is played by an actor. The experiment is in reality to see how far the teacher will go in giving electric shocks of increasing voltage when told to do so by a man in a white coat.

What shocked the young man, the now famous Stanley Milgram, was that most subjects carried on the experiment to the end, to a voltage high enough to fell a horse, in the face of the (feigned) agonised screams of the learner. And who can blame him. Remember these subjects were not selected to be particularly pliable. They were simply whoever walked in off the street willing to give an hour of their time for a small amount of money, a mere four dollars. Two thirds of normal, everyday people would be ready to torture a stranger to death, within earshot of his cries for mercy, just because a man in a white coat told them it was in the interest of science. Oh and as long as the subject is invisible, separated by a simple screen or a thin partition wall.

In the secret footage of Winterbourne View possibly the most horrifying aspect is that most of the abuse happens in full view of all the other residents and staff. As one helpless, and often bubblingly happy, girl is pinned beneath a chair with her arm forced up behind her back, in obvious agony, others wander past, while one 'care-worker' (I use the term loosely, you understand) covers her head with a blanket. Provided the events are hidden, he almost seems to be saying, then anything goes. In his original findings, Milgram notes that, where the learner was visible, similarly the teacher could not look at them, averting eyes, shielding face, avoiding any contact, even denigrating or demonising the learner so as to put distance between themselves and responsibility for their actions.

Milgram's conclusions focused on the willingness of ordinary people to obey authority. He was trying to discover the degree to which the Nazi perpetrators' defence that they were just obeying orders was valid. His conclusion seems to be simple. An oppressive, murderous regime will have no trouble finding enough people ready to do its bidding, even when those self-same people would genuinely abhor such behaviour in themselves or others. Under the right conditions most of us would murder our neighbour. The jury is out as to why. Are we so morally weak? Do we have some kind of social survival instinct that over-rules everything else? Is morality as we generally see it far more rare than we'd like to think, reserved for a brave few?

I have no idea why and I'm not sure anyone else does. But I cannot forget it is my son out there whom society will quietly neglect. Even if a few care for his welfare, even if all those who know him will love him, the wind of the world is against him. Somehow we have come to live in a culture that worships perfection and isolates inadequacy.

I know one reason. We accept as normal the idea that the invisible, disabled, human, nonperson, has no right to our protection, and may be disposed of at will. No one stands up to argue for equality in the womb for the disabled. It is abhorrent to dispose of your womb dweller if she happens to have a second X chromosome, but perfectly acceptable if he happens to have an extra chromosome 21. We shout 'equality' for the born loudly from the rafters but inequality for the unborn is a matter of public policy.

I do not mean by this that institutions are necessarily bad, or that the individuals in them bear no moral responsibility. I'm merely offering the thought that they tend to follow trend. They act as a weathervane of the prevailing wind of culture, which remains quietly discriminatory to the disabled, secretly demeaning to the weak and vulnerable.

I have another reason for believing that institutions of whatever form are not the place for Caleb. I was institutionalised at twelve years old and have been recovering ever since. 'My name's George and I'm a boarder' or at least I was. I returned recently to my alma mater (what a strange phrase that is) and was asked what it was like in my day. 'A form of institutionalised bullying' was my swift and heartfelt reply. The odd thing is this: I was one of the successful ones. A school hero in my first term through winning the cross-country race, top at maths and science, in endless school teams, and well liked, nay even respected. Nauseating but true. I was one of those annoying gits who was good at everything – someone should have put me down as a service to the community. But I was bullied by the system and in turn I bullied others.

At the end of the first term, on returning home, I found that my mother had decided we were old enough to help around the house and constructed a list of jobs. The screams could have been heard in the next county. I wailed and raged and smashed. To her eternal credit she just ripped up the list. What she did not know (and how did parents in those days allow themselves to be so ignorant of what really went on?) was that I had spent four months on a list. This list told me all the jobs I had to do. Clean prefects' studies before they got up. Stay in the study hall in break so they could ring a bell (can you believe it?) for me to run down to their studies to make them toast or tea. Tidy this, clean that, and transport the other. I had no time to call my own, no space to escape into and no one who cared one tiny little ounce what became of me. The housemaster was a genial old fart, who, in his soft and gentle way, would probably have noticed if I'd disappeared, eventually, but as to whether I was happy? You might have just as well asked him what the weather was like on Mars. The most senior boys ran the house. They were not cruel, in fact quite reformatory after their own worse experiences when they were our age. They were just boys and so, in the end, it became the survival of the toughest.

In spite of my luck in being good at stuff, I also had to stand up for myself. One group of boys, just two years senior to us, were merciless thugs, and you had to avoid being a target. So I grew a thick skin, developed a sharp tongue and exploded if anyone lower down the pecking order spoke back. One boy particularly became the butt of my jokes and I am sure I made his life utterly miserable. We shared a name and, with hindsight, I suspect I felt I had to distance myself from him (he was definitely not a success story), so I picked on him. This is to my undying shame and I would love to be able to say sorry. He had a miserable life. I suspect it would have been pretty awful without me, but I certainly made it worse.

Of course school had its highlights, I don't mean scoring winning tries, winning races, getting prizes. These happen to the lucky but aren't the stuff of real life, for only the privileged few can taste them. No, the real highlights were the mistakes. My best moment was standing in the middle of a cloud of sulphuric acid fumes after a teacher had just blown up my experiment. Only the shattered base of a large jar was left as all around students picked bits of glass from jackets and trousers, off benches and out of beakers.

Almost as good was when another, truly incompetent, teacher broke a vial of bromine on a lab bench. The room had to be evacuated, with one student dragged out by his feet and the teacher in question, known universally as The Vegetable or Veg, was rushed off to hospital with sirens blazing. A short while later a lowly paid lab assistant did the same experiment, briefly, without fuss, with a quiet resigned look on his face, which told all the world that he knew he was a talented man working for morons.

Climbing on roofs, having your naked butt photographed on the prefects' hallowed grass, snogging in the bushes (we had girls, before you ask), breaking endless bones in rugby (stupid game), cycling ten miles in the dark with no lights just to get a drink in a pub, chilblains (surprisingly unpleasant), all these were part of the fun. But it was always an institution.

At about the same time that Stanley Milgram was conducting his experiments, a slightly older academic called Jean Vanier* was introduced to some adult men with mental disabilities. He recalls later how he had difficulty communicating with them but that each one showed as much through body language as through words that what he wanted was relationship. 'Will you come back?' was all they seemed to ask. He contrasted this with his philosophy students whose focus was always on ideas. He then noted a second question that underlay the others. 'Why am I like this? Why have I been abandoned?' As Vanier puts it, 'there is something incomprehensible about finding yourself on this earth and nobody wanting you.' A little later he met two orphaned men with learning difficulties, as we call it today, and asked them to come and live with him, and so L'Arche was borne.

L'Arche means The Ark, a reminder of Noah's Ark, where people are welcomed in to escape from the flood. As Vanier puts it, 'many disabled people are caught up in the flood, killed off because they're not wanted, killed before birth, killed after birth, [or] shoved into institutions'. He argues that disabled people have a message for us. They are not capable of doing great things but they have a power of cooperation and communication. At L'Arche every meal is a banquet, for everyone has an equal place at the table. It was a dream I wanted to explore for myself. So I booked myself into a week joining with a L'Arche community. Just to see. Could this be Caleb's future?

I don't know but I do know that as I pondered my visit I began to regret my rant about bullying. Until, that is, I listened to the radio. As I listened I heard that a young man had just walked into a primary school and shot dead five teachers and as many young children as he could find, before turning the guns on himself. It was a time for tears again, but also a time for anger, and bemusement. How could a country tolerate unrestricted access to guns and ammunition? In some States in America you can buy them in some supermarkets as if they are cans of beans. What drove a young man to do such a thing? He was apparently sensitive and thoughtful – hardly the usual characteristics of a mass murderer. And, most bizarrely, why on earth did his mother feel safer in a secure rural neighbourhood with four guns and hundreds of round of ammunition in her basement? It seems to me a bit like keeping a bomb in the basement in case World War Three breaks out. Blowing yourself up is a little higher up the probability ladder.

While all are most concerned about the families, the political focus has so far been on the guns, but there is a dissenting voice. In her book The Bully Society an American academic called Jessie Klein argues that American public schools are a place of routine bullying, which goes largely unchallenged by those in authority. The sensitive and vulnerable are traumatised and the aggressive and confident are inured to cruelty such that either may erupt in unrestricted violence. The easy access to guns and the combat training through computer games allow such violence to spawn death on a grand scale, and so those who create and sell them are not immune from blame, but the root is in the institutions. This may explain why these atrocities are so often targeted at schools rather than other more obvious public spaces. It's a form of unfocused revenge. Truly institutionalised violence.

At L'Arche it was striking how unlike an institution the whole set up felt. In one way, it was gloriously amateur, of the 'what shall we do next' variety. Everything was planned, of course, and everyone was safety checked to the utmost degree. But you didn't feel that there were lists of targets to achieve or goals to reach. One core member could not see enough to recognise anything much, could not write, had pretty much no short-term memory, and yet he played a full part in a lesson. He achieved, and everyone valued it, but it made no difference to how we treated him. He was just a lovely guy who turned up with a huge cross around his neck, couldn't wait for the next break and asked you your name every five minutes.

In another way it was just like a family. I mean a proper one – messy and fun, uncomfortable and familiar. Even to the extent that certain members appeared to unconsciously adopt the role of father or mother. Not necessarily the fully mentally able, either. In one house the longest resident was so much Dad that you almost expected the pipe and slippers to be brought out. He tended to have snot dripping off his nose and he dribbled great big globs of goo when he talked to you, but he was Dad – or 'just like my Dad' as my daughter might say. He was also an international speaker, by the way, and when he spoke people listened. Caleb would fit in a treat. He'd cause a riot but he is the ideal family member. He cannot bear it if people fall out, cares for every cut and bruise and makes everyone laugh until it hurts.

Yesterday Caleb added to his Christmas list. He asked for a dog basket. Not, you understand, for a dog, but for himself. He wanted one to sleep in. We did seriously consider buying him one, even going so far as to check them out for size at the local market. But when it came to it, we just couldn't do it. 'What does it say about Caleb?' was Alison's thought. 'What would social services say?' was mine. He'd love it and probably sleep in it at night, but it just didn't seem right.

I'm not sure why I told that story, but it kept me amused for a while, just the thought of him curled up under a blanket. And it reminds me of what Caleb has taught me. He's taught me not to be a bully; that real vulnerability draws out gentleness and love, not violence and a desire to dominate. When he really loses control of his emotions usually all I have to do is hold him close and say 'I understand' over and over again and he settles down. I never got that at school and you will never get that in an institution. And it's what the really vulnerable need. But it's also what the strong need. They need to have drawn out from them the generosity and affection required by the vulnerable. Only then can both find identity and community. Here's the future I hope for Caleb.

And that's it. Not such a big idea but maybe an important one. Getting rid of womb dwellers like Caleb is not so much bad as foolish. Why? Well, it is not really so awful for them for they never know any better. It may even be said, as C S Lewis puts it, that God is most interested in populating heaven so we do not need to worry about the womb dwellers at all. No, it is really and truly awful for us. It makes us hard and cold and careless. Without them it is we who die inside. With them we grow truly kind. Or to put it simply, 'Everyone needs a Caleb'. Not out there, in some institution, but in here, right next to us. In our families, in our homes, in our streets and in our towns, everyone needs a Caleb.

by the same author…

Look Up in Lockdown
In the Coronavirus Crisis:
A Country Vicar's Blog

…more overleaf

If you've enjoyed this, then try the author's other works, also found on Amazon, including *Look up in Lockdown: In the Coronavirus Crisis: a Country Vicar's Blog.*

God is not silent
The Word of the Lord came to Joel (Joel 1:1)
Day 1 : 16 Mar 2020

I often wonder what this might have felt like. Did Joel fall into a trance? Did he have a dream? Or was it more a kind of waking certainty that God had something important he wanted Joel to pass on?

I rather suspect the latter. He knew as he looked at the tragedy unfolding around him, that God had no desire to stay silent. His God had an important message to share and Joel was going to be the means to share it.

Now, I am not convinced by those today who claim some divine hotline into the meaning of current events. It's usually hard to see why God would pass such vital information on to them. But I am convinced that God does not leave us without a witness, without some meaning to the affairs that have such an impact on our lives. God wants us to hear his voice in the big things as well as the little, in the global as well as the everyday.

So as we ponder the spread of a new and virulent virus for which we have no immunity, what might God be saying to us? Well that's the question of this blog. As many find they have extra time on their hands to listen to God, is there something God wants to say? I am not claiming any special insight, of course, but rather a willingness to explore, together with anyone who wishes to travel with me, God's perspective and God's heart when we find ourselves and our world in crisis. Do come with me.

So begins a series of blogs that follow the spread and retreat of the virus, the fickle actions of politicians and the personal experiences of the author through this strangest of times. Each one held together by words of the Old Testament prophet Joel, who faced a similar calamity and saw God's hand in it.

*As some of you will know, it appears Jean Vanier had a darker side to his life. While the work with those with additional needs remains a bright light in the world, his treatment of a number of women under his thrall is a very different chapter. I am sure that there are lessons that we need to learn from this which are beyond the scope of this book but I am glad that the work he started seems to have been able to grow beyond his legacy. It, at least, continues to bring hope and happiness to all those who live in L'Arche communities.

Printed in Great Britain
by Amazon

37245831R00081